To a top researcher
and good friend,
Bart

Analytics in a Big Data World

Wiley & SAS Business Series

The Wiley & SAS Business Series presents books that help senior-level managers with their critical management decisions.

Titles in the Wiley & SAS Business Series include:

Activity-Based Management for Financial Institutions: Driving Bottom-Line Results by Brent Bahnub

Bank Fraud: Using Technology to Combat Losses by Revathi Subramanian

Big Data Analytics: Turning Big Data into Big Money by Frank Ohlhorst

Branded! How Retailers Engage Consumers with Social Media and Mobility by Bernie Brennan and Lori Schafer

Business Analytics for Customer Intelligence by Gert Laursen

Business Analytics for Managers: Taking Business Intelligence beyond Reporting by Gert Laursen and Jesper Thorlund

The Business Forecasting Deal: Exposing Bad Practices and Providing Practical Solutions by Michael Gilliland

Business Intelligence Applied: Implementing an Effective Information and Communications Technology Infrastructure by Michael Gendron

Business Intelligence in the Cloud: Strategic Implementation Guide by Michael S. Gendron

Business Intelligence Success Factors: Tools for Aligning Your Business in the Global Economy by Olivia Parr Rud

CIO Best Practices: Enabling Strategic Value with Information Technology, second edition by Joe Stenzel

Connecting Organizational Silos: Taking Knowledge Flow Management to the Next Level with Social Media by Frank Leistner

Credit Risk Assessment: The New Lending System for Borrowers, Lenders, and Investors by Clark Abrahams and Mingyuan Zhang

Killer Analytics: Top 20 Metrics Missing from Your Balance Sheet by Mark Brown

Manufacturing Best Practices: Optimizing Productivity and Product Quality by Bobby Hull

Marketing Automation: Practical Steps to More Effective Direct Marketing by Jeff LeSueur

Mastering Organizational Knowledge Flow: How to Make Knowledge Sharing Work by Frank Leistner

The New Know: Innovation Powered by Analytics by Thornton May

Performance Management: Integrating Strategy Execution, Methodologies, Risk, and Analytics by Gary Cokins

Predictive Business Analytics: Forward-Looking Capabilities to Improve Business Performance by Lawrence Maisel and Gary Cokins

Retail Analytics: The Secret Weapon by Emmett Cox

Social Network Analysis in Telecommunications by Carlos Andre Reis Pinheiro

Statistical Thinking: Improving Business Performance, second edition by Roger W. Hoerl and Ronald D. Snee

Taming the Big Data Tidal Wave: Finding Opportunities in Huge Data Streams with Advanced Analytics by Bill Franks

Too Big to Ignore: The Business Case for Big Data by Phil Simon

The Value of Business Analytics: Identifying the Path to Profitability by Evan Stubbs

Visual Six Sigma: Making Data Analysis Lean by Ian Cox, Marie A. Gaudard, Philip J. Ramsey, Mia L. Stephens, and Leo Wright

Win with Advanced Business Analytics: Creating Business Value from Your Data by Jean Paul Isson and Jesse Harriott

For more information on any of the above titles, please visit www.wiley.com.

Analytics in a Big Data World

The Essential Guide to Data Science and Its Applications

Bart Baesens

Published by John Wiley & Sons, Inc., Hoboken, New Jersey.
Published simultaneously in Canada.

For general information on our other products and services or for technical support, please contact our Customer Care Department within the United States at (800) 762-2974, outside the United States at (317) 572-3993 or fax (317) 572-4002.

Wiley publishes in a variety of print and electronic formats and by print-on-demand. Some material included with standard print versions of this book may not be included in e-books or in print-on-demand. If this book refers to media such as a CD or DVD that is not included in the version you purchased, you may download this material at http://booksupport.wiley.com. For more information about Wiley products, visit www.wiley.com.

Library of Congress Cataloging-in-Publication Data:
Baesens, Bart.
    Analytics in a big data world : the essential guide to data science and its applications / Bart Baesens.
      1 online resource. — (Wiley & SAS business series)
    Description based on print version record and CIP data provided by publisher; resource not viewed.
      ISBN 978-1-118-89271-8 (ebk); ISBN 978-1-118-89274-9 (ebk);
    ISBN 978-1-118-89270-1 (cloth)   1. Big data.   2. Management—Statistical methods.   3. Management—Data processing.   4. Decision making—Data processing.   I. Title.
      HD30.215
      658.4'038   dc23
                                                                    2014004728

Printed in the United States of America

10 9 8 7 6 5 4 3 2 1

To my wonderful wife, Katrien, and my kids,
Ann-Sophie, Victor, and Hannelore.
To my parents and parents-in-law.

Contents

Preface

Companies are being flooded with tsunamis of data collected in a multichannel business environment, leaving an untapped potential for analytics to better understand, manage, and strategically exploit the complex dynamics of customer behavior. In this book, we will discuss how analytics can be used to create strategic leverage and identify new business opportunities.

The focus of this book is not on the mathematics or theory, but on the practical application. Formulas and equations will only be included when absolutely needed from a practitioner's perspective. It is also not our aim to provide exhaustive coverage of all analytical techniques previously developed, but rather to cover the ones that really provide added value in a business setting.

The book is written in a condensed, focused way because it is targeted at the business professional. A reader's prerequisite knowledge should consist of some basic exposure to descriptive statistics (e.g., mean, standard deviation, correlation, confidence intervals, hypothesis testing), data handling (using, for example, Microsoft Excel, SQL, etc.), and data visualization (e.g., bar plots, pie charts, histograms, scatter plots). Throughout the book, many examples of real-life case studies will be included in areas such as risk management, fraud detection, customer relationship management, web analytics, and so forth. The author will also integrate both his research and consulting experience throughout the various chapters. The book is aimed at senior data analysts, consultants, analytics practitioners, and PhD researchers starting to explore the field.

Chapter 1 discusses big data and analytics. It starts with some example application areas, followed by an overview of the analytics process model and job profiles involved, and concludes by discussing key analytic model requirements. Chapter 2 provides an overview of data collection, sampling, and preprocessing. Data is the key ingredient to any analytical exercise, hence the importance of this chapter. It discusses sampling, types of data elements, visual data exploration and exploratory statistical analysis, missing values, outlier detection and treatment, standardizing data, categorization, weights of evidence coding, variable selection, and segmentation. Chapter 3 discusses predictive analytics. It starts with an overview of the target definition and then continues to discuss various analytics techniques such as linear regression, logistic regression, decision trees, neural networks, support vector machines, and ensemble methods (bagging, boosting, random forests). In addition, multiclass classification techniques are covered, such as multiclass logistic regression, multiclass decision trees, multiclass neural networks, and multiclass support vector machines. The chapter concludes by discussing the evaluation of predictive models. Chapter 4 covers descriptive analytics. First, association rules are discussed that aim at discovering intratransaction patterns. This is followed by a section on sequence rules that aim at discovering intertransaction patterns. Segmentation techniques are also covered. Chapter 5 introduces survival analysis. The chapter starts by introducing some key survival analysis measurements. This is followed by a discussion of Kaplan Meier analysis, parametric survival analysis, and proportional hazards regression. The chapter concludes by discussing various extensions and evaluation of survival analysis models. Chapter 6 covers social network analytics. The chapter starts by discussing example social network applications. Next, social network definitions and metrics are given. This is followed by a discussion on social network learning. The relational neighbor classifier and its probabilistic variant together with relational logistic regression are covered next. The chapter ends by discussing egonets and bigraphs. Chapter 7 provides an overview of key activities to be considered when putting analytics to work. It starts with a recapitulation of the analytic model requirements and then continues with a discussion of backtesting, benchmarking, data quality, software, privacy, model design and documentation, and corporate governance. Chapter 8 concludes the book by discussing various example applications such as credit risk modeling, fraud detection, net lift response modeling, churn prediction, recommender systems, web analytics, social media analytics, and business process analytics.

Acknowledgments

I would like to acknowledge all my colleagues who contributed to this text: Seppe vanden Broucke, Alex Seret, Thomas Verbraken, Aimée Backiel, Véronique Van Vlasselaer, Helen Moges, and Barbara Dergent.

Analytics in a Big Data World

CHAPTER 1

Big Data and Analytics

D ata are everywhere. IBM projects that every day we generate 2.5 quintillion bytes of data.[1] In relative terms, this means 90 percent of the data in the world has been created in the last two years. Gartner projects that by 2015, 85 percent of Fortune 500 organizations will be unable to exploit big data for competitive advantage and about 4.4 million jobs will be created around big data.[2] Although these estimates should not be interpreted in an absolute sense, they are a strong indication of the ubiquity of big data and the strong need for analytical skills and resources because, as the data piles up, managing and analyzing these data resources in the most optimal way become critical success factors in creating competitive advantage and strategic leverage.

Figure 1.1 shows the results of a KDnuggets[3] poll conducted during April 2013 about the largest data sets analyzed. The total number of respondents was 322 and the numbers per category are indicated between brackets. The median was estimated to be in the 40 to 50 gigabyte (GB) range, which was about double the median answer for a similar poll run in 2012 (20 to 40 GB). This clearly shows the quick increase in size of data that analysts are working on. A further regional breakdown of the poll showed that U.S. data miners lead other regions in big data, with about 28% of them working with terabyte (TB) size databases.

A main obstacle to fully harnessing the power of big data using analytics is the lack of skilled resources and "data scientist" talent required to

Less than 1 MB (12)	3.7%
1.1 to 10 MB (8)	2.5%
11 to 100 MB (14)	4.3%
101 MB to 1 GB (50)	15.5%
1.1 to 10 GB (59)	18%
11 to 100 GB (52)	16%
101 GB to 1 TB (59)	18%
1.1 to 10 TB (39)	12%
11 to 100 TB (15)	4.7%
101 TB to 1 PB (6)	1.9%
1.1 to 10 PB (2)	0.6%
11 to 100 PB (0)	0%
Over 100 PB (6)	1.9%

Figure 1.1   Results from a KDnuggets Poll about Largest Data Sets Analyzed
Source: www.kdnuggets.com/polls/2013/largest-dataset-analyzed-data-mined-2013.html.

exploit big data. In another poll ran by KDnuggets in July 2013, a strong need emerged for analytics/big data/data mining/data science education.[4] It is the purpose of this book to try and fill this gap by providing a concise and focused overview of analytics for the business practitioner.

EXAMPLE APPLICATIONS

Analytics is everywhere and strongly embedded into our daily lives. As I am writing this part, I was the subject of various analytical models today. When I checked my physical mailbox this morning, I found a catalogue sent to me most probably as a result of a response modeling analytical exercise that indicated that, given my characteristics and previous purchase behavior, I am likely to buy one or more products from it. Today, I was the subject of a behavioral scoring model of my financial institution. This is a model that will look at, among other things, my checking account balance from the past 12 months and my credit payments during that period, together with other kinds of information available to my bank, to predict whether I will default on my loan during the next year. My bank needs to know this for provisioning purposes. Also today, my telephone services provider analyzed my calling behavior and my account information to predict whether I will churn during the next three months. As I logged on to my Facebook page, the social ads appearing there were based on analyzing all information (posts, pictures, my friends and their behavior, etc.) available to Facebook. My Twitter posts will be analyzed (possibly in real time) by social media analytics to understand both the subject of my tweets and the sentiment of them. As I checked out in the supermarket, my loyalty card was scanned first, followed by all my purchases. This will be used by my supermarket to analyze my market basket, which will help it decide on product bundling, next best offer, improving shelf organization, and so forth. As I made the payment with my credit card, my credit card provider used a fraud detection model to see whether it was a legitimate transaction. When I receive my credit card statement later, it will be accompanied by various vouchers that are the result of an analytical customer segmentation exercise to better understand my expense behavior.

To summarize, the relevance, importance, and impact of analytics are now bigger than ever before and, given that more and more data are being collected and that there is strategic value in knowing what is hidden in data, analytics will continue to grow. Without claiming to be exhaustive, Table 1.1 presents some examples of how analytics is applied in various settings.

Table 1.1 Example Analytics Applications

Marketing	Risk Management	Government	Web	Logistics	Other
Response modeling	Credit risk modeling	Tax avoidance	Web analytics	Demand forecasting	Text analytics
Net lift modeling	Market risk modeling	Social security fraud	Social media analytics	Supply chain analytics	Business process analytics
Retention modeling	Operational risk modeling	Money laundering	Multivariate testing		
Market basket analysis	Fraud detection	Terrorism detection			
Recommender systems					
Customer segmentation					

It is the purpose of this book to discuss the underlying techniques and key challenges to work out the applications shown in Table 1.1 using analytics. Some of these applications will be discussed in further detail in Chapter 8.

BASIC NOMENCLATURE

In order to start doing analytics, some basic vocabulary needs to be defined. A first important concept here concerns the basic unit of analysis. Customers can be considered from various perspectives. Customer lifetime value (CLV) can be measured for either individual customers or at the household level. Another alternative is to look at account behavior. For example, consider a credit scoring exercise for which the aim is to predict whether the applicant will default on a particular mortgage loan account. The analysis can also be done at the transaction level. For example, in insurance fraud detection, one usually performs the analysis at insurance claim level. Also, in web analytics, the basic unit of analysis is usually a web visit or session.

It is also important to note that customers can play different roles. For example, parents can buy goods for their kids, such that there is a clear distinction between the payer and the end user. In a banking setting, a customer can be primary account owner, secondary account owner, main debtor of the credit, codebtor, guarantor, and so on. It is very important to clearly distinguish between those different roles when defining and/or aggregating data for the analytics exercise.

Finally, in case of predictive analytics, the target variable needs to be appropriately defined. For example, when is a customer considered to be a churner or not, a fraudster or not, a responder or not, or how should the CLV be appropriately defined?

ANALYTICS PROCESS MODEL

Figure 1.2 gives a high-level overview of the analytics process model.[5] As a first step, a thorough definition of the business problem to be solved with analytics is needed. Next, all source data need to be identified that could be of potential interest. This is a very important step, as data is the key ingredient to any analytical exercise and the selection of data will have a deterministic impact on the analytical models that will be built in a subsequent step. All data will then be gathered in a staging area, which could be, for example, a data mart or data warehouse. Some basic exploratory analysis can be considered here using, for example, online analytical processing (OLAP) facilities for multidimensional data analysis (e.g., roll-up, drill down, slicing and dicing). This will be followed by a data cleaning step to get rid of all inconsistencies, such as missing values, outliers, and duplicate data. Additional transformations may also be considered, such as binning, alphanumeric to numeric coding, geographical aggregation, and so forth. In the analytics step, an analytical model will be estimated on the preprocessed and transformed data. Different types of analytics can be considered here (e.g., to do churn prediction, fraud detection, customer segmentation, market basket analysis). Finally, once the model has been built, it will be interpreted and evaluated by the business experts. Usually, many trivial patterns will be detected by the model. For example, in a market basket analysis setting, one may find that spaghetti and spaghetti sauce are often purchased together. These patterns are interesting because they provide some validation of the model. But of course, the key issue here is to find the unexpected yet interesting and actionable patterns (sometimes also referred to as *knowledge diamonds*) that can provide added value in the business setting. Once the analytical model has been appropriately validated and approved, it can be put into production as an analytics application (e.g., decision support system, scoring engine). It is important to consider here how to represent the model output in a user-friendly way, how to integrate it with other applications (e.g., campaign management tools, risk engines), and how to make sure the analytical model can be appropriately monitored and backtested on an ongoing basis.

It is important to note that the process model outlined in Figure 1.2 is iterative in nature, in the sense that one may have to go back to previous steps during the exercise. For example, during the analytics step, the need for additional data may be identified, which may necessitate additional cleaning, transformation, and so forth. Also, the most time consuming step is the data selection and preprocessing step; this usually takes around 80% of the total efforts needed to build an analytical model.

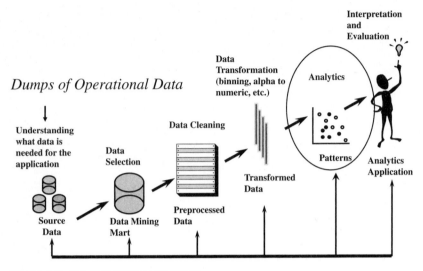

Figure 1.2 The Analytics Process Model

JOB PROFILES INVOLVED

Analytics is essentially a multidisciplinary exercise in which many different job profiles need to collaborate together. In what follows, we will discuss the most important job profiles.

The database or data warehouse administrator (DBA) is aware of all the data available within the firm, the storage details, and the data definitions. Hence, the DBA plays a crucial role in feeding the analytical modeling exercise with its key ingredient, which is data. Because analytics is an iterative exercise, the DBA may continue to play an important role as the modeling exercise proceeds.

Another very important profile is the business expert. This could, for example, be a credit portfolio manager, fraud detection expert, brand manager, or e-commerce manager. This person has extensive business experience and business common sense, which is very valuable. It is precisely this knowledge that will help to steer the analytical modeling exercise and interpret its key findings. A key challenge here is that much of the expert knowledge is tacit and may be hard to elicit at the start of the modeling exercise.

Legal experts are becoming more and more important given that not all data can be used in an analytical model because of privacy, discrimination, and so forth. For example, in credit risk modeling, one can typically not discriminate good and bad customers based upon gender, national origin, or religion. In web analytics, information is typically gathered by means of cookies, which are files that are stored on the user's browsing computer. However, when gathering information using cookies, users should be appropriately informed. This is subject to regulation at various levels (both national and, for example, European). A key challenge here is that privacy and other regulation highly vary depending on the geographical region. Hence, the legal expert should have good knowledge about what data can be used when, and what regulation applies in what location.

The data scientist, data miner, or data analyst is the person responsible for doing the actual analytics. This person should possess a thorough understanding of all techniques involved and know how to implement them using the appropriate software. A good data scientist should also have good communication and presentation skills to report the analytical findings back to the other parties involved.

The software tool vendors should also be mentioned as an important part of the analytics team. Different types of tool vendors can be distinguished here. Some vendors only provide tools to automate specific steps of the analytical modeling process (e.g., data preprocessing). Others sell software that covers the entire analytical modeling process. Some vendors also provide analytics-based solutions for specific application areas, such as risk management, marketing analytics and campaign management, and so on.

ANALYTICS

Analytics is a term that is often used interchangeably with *data science, data mining, knowledge discovery,* and others. The distinction between all those is not clear cut. All of these terms essentially refer to extracting useful business patterns or mathematical decision models from a preprocessed data set. Different underlying techniques can be used for this purpose, stemming from a variety of different disciplines, such as:

- Statistics (e.g., linear and logistic regression)
- Machine learning (e.g., decision trees)

- Biology (e.g., neural networks, genetic algorithms, swarm intelligence)
- Kernel methods (e.g., support vector machines)

Basically, a distinction can be made between predictive and descriptive analytics. In predictive analytics, a target variable is typically available, which can either be categorical (e.g., churn or not, fraud or not) or continuous (e.g., customer lifetime value, loss given default). In descriptive analytics, no such target variable is available. Common examples here are association rules, sequence rules, and clustering. Figure 1.3 provides an example of a decision tree in a classification predictive analytics setting for predicting churn.

More than ever before, analytical models steer the strategic risk decisions of companies. For example, in a bank setting, the minimum equity and provisions a financial institution holds are directly determined by, among other things, credit risk analytics, market risk analytics, operational risk analytics, fraud analytics, and insurance risk analytics. In this setting, analytical model errors directly affect profitability, solvency, shareholder value, the macroeconomy, and society as a whole. Hence, it is of the utmost importance that analytical

Customer	Age	Recency	Frequency	Monetary	Churn
John	35	5	6	100	Yes
Sophie	18	10	2	150	No
Victor	38	28	8	20	No
Laura	44	12	4	280	Yes

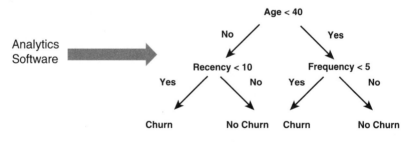

Figure 1.3 Example of Classification Predictive Analytics

models are developed in the most optimal way, taking into account various requirements that will be discussed in what follows.

ANALYTICAL MODEL REQUIREMENTS

A good analytical model should satisfy several requirements, depending on the application area. A first critical success factor is business relevance. The analytical model should actually solve the business problem for which it was developed. It makes no sense to have a working analytical model that got sidetracked from the original problem statement. In order to achieve business relevance, it is of key importance that the business problem to be solved is appropriately defined, qualified, and agreed upon by all parties involved at the outset of the analysis.

A second criterion is statistical performance. The model should have statistical significance and predictive power. How this can be measured will depend upon the type of analytics considered. For example, in a classification setting (churn, fraud), the model should have good discrimination power. In a clustering setting, the clusters should be as homogenous as possible. In later chapters, we will extensively discuss various measures to quantify this.

Depending on the application, analytical models should also be interpretable and justifiable. *Interpretability* refers to understanding the patterns that the analytical model captures. This aspect has a certain degree of subjectivism, since interpretability may depend on the business user's knowledge. In many settings, however, it is considered to be a key requirement. For example, in credit risk modeling or medical diagnosis, interpretable models are absolutely needed to get good insight into the underlying data patterns. In other settings, such as response modeling and fraud detection, having interpretable models may be less of an issue. *Justifiability* refers to the degree to which a model corresponds to prior business knowledge and intuition.[6] For example, a model stating that a higher debt ratio results in more creditworthy clients may be interpretable, but is not justifiable because it contradicts basic financial intuition. Note that both interpretability and justifiability often need to be balanced against statistical performance. Often one will observe that high performing analytical models are incomprehensible and black box in nature. A popular example of this is neural networks, which are universal approximators and are high performing, but offer no insight into the underlying patterns in the data. On the contrary, linear regression models are very transparent and comprehensible, but offer only limited modeling power.

Analytical models should also be *operationally efficient*. This refers to the efforts needed to collect the data, preprocess it, evaluate the model, and feed its outputs to the business application (e.g., campaign management, capital calculation). Especially in a real-time online scoring environment (e.g., fraud detection) this may be a crucial characteristic. Operational efficiency also entails the efforts needed to monitor and backtest the model, and reestimate it when necessary.

Another key attention point is the *economic cost* needed to set up the analytical model. This includes the costs to gather and preprocess the data, the costs to analyze the data, and the costs to put the resulting analytical models into production. In addition, the software costs and human and computing resources should be taken into account here. It is important to do a thorough cost–benefit analysis at the start of the project.

Finally, analytical models should also comply with both local and international *regulation and legislation*. For example, in a credit risk setting, the Basel II and Basel III Capital Accords have been introduced to appropriately identify the types of data that can or cannot be used to build credit risk models. In an insurance setting, the Solvency II Accord plays a similar role. Given the importance of analytics nowadays, more and more regulation is being introduced relating to the development and use of the analytical models. In addition, in the context of privacy, many new regulatory developments are taking place at various levels. A popular example here concerns the use of cookies in a web analytics context.

NOTES

1. IBM, www.ibm.com/big-data/us/en, 2013.
2. www.gartner.com/technology/topics/big-data.jsp.
3. www.kdnuggets.com/polls/2013/largest-dataset-analyzed-data-mined-2013.html.
4. www.kdnuggets.com/polls/2013/analytics-data-science-education.html.

5. J. Han and M. Kamber, *Data Mining: Concepts and Techniques,* 2nd ed. (Morgan Kaufmann, Waltham, MA, US, 2006); D. J. Hand, H. Mannila, and P. Smyth, *Principles of Data Mining* (MIT Press, Cambridge, Massachusetts, London, England, 2001); P. N. Tan, M. Steinbach, and V. Kumar, *Introduction to Data Mining* (Pearson, Upper Saddle River, New Jersey, US, 2006).

6. D. Martens, J. Vanthienen, W. Verbeke, and B. Baesens, "Performance of Classification Models from a User Perspective." Special issue, *Decision Support Systems* 51, no. 4 (2011): 782–793.

CHAPTER 2

Data Collection, Sampling, and Preprocessing

D ata are key ingredients for any analytical exercise. Hence, it is important to thoroughly consider and list all data sources that are of potential interest before starting the analysis. The rule here is the more data, the better. However, real life data can be dirty because of inconsistencies, incompleteness, duplication, and merging problems. Throughout the analytical modeling steps, various data filtering mechanisms will be applied to clean up and reduce the data to a manageable and relevant size. Worth mentioning here is the garbage in, garbage out (GIGO) principle, which essentially states that messy data will yield messy analytical models. It is of the utmost importance that every data preprocessing step is carefully justified, carried out, validated, and documented before proceeding with further analysis. Even the slightest mistake can make the data totally unusable for further analysis. In what follows, we will elaborate on the most important data preprocessing steps that should be considered during an analytical modeling exercise.

TYPES OF DATA SOURCES

As previously mentioned, more data is better to start off the analysis. Data can originate from a variety of different sources, which will be explored in what follows.

Transactions are the first important source of data. Transactional data consist of structured, low-level, detailed information capturing the key characteristics of a customer transaction (e.g., purchase, claim, cash transfer, credit card payment). This type of data is usually stored in massive online transaction processing (OLTP) relational databases. It can also be summarized over longer time horizons by aggregating it into averages, absolute/relative trends, maximum/minimum values, and so on.

Unstructured data embedded in text documents (e.g., emails, web pages, claim forms) or multimedia content can also be interesting to analyze. However, these sources typically require extensive preprocessing before they can be successfully included in an analytical exercise.

Another important source of data is qualitative, expert-based data. An expert is a person with a substantial amount of subject matter expertise within a particular setting (e.g., credit portfolio manager, brand manager). The expertise stems from both common sense and business experience, and it is important to elicit expertise as much as possible before the analytics is run. This will steer the modeling in the right direction and allow you to interpret the analytical results from the right perspective. A popular example of applying expert-based validation is checking the univariate signs of a regression model. For example, one would expect *a priori* that higher debt has an adverse impact on credit risk, such that it should have a negative sign in the final scorecard. If this turns out not to be the case (e.g., due to bad data quality, multicollinearity), the expert/business user will not be tempted to use the analytical model at all, since it contradicts prior expectations.

Nowadays, data poolers are becoming more and more important in the industry. Popular examples are Dun & Bradstreet, Bureau Van Dijck, and Thomson Reuters. The core business of these companies is to gather data in a particular setting (e.g., credit risk, marketing), build models with it, and sell the output of these models (e.g., scores), possibly together with the underlying raw data, to interested customers. A popular example of this in the United States is the FICO score, which is a credit score ranging between 300 and 850 that is provided by the three most important credit bureaus: Experian, Equifax, and Transunion. Many financial institutions use these FICO scores either as their final internal model, or as a benchmark against an internally developed credit scorecard to better understand the weaknesses of the latter.

Finally, plenty of publicly available data can be included in the analytical exercise. A first important example is macroeconomic data about gross domestic product (GDP), inflation, unemployment, and so on. By including this type of data in an analytical model, it will become possible to see how the model varies with the state of the economy. This is especially relevant in a credit risk setting, where typically all models need to be thoroughly stress tested. In addition, social media data from Facebook, Twitter, and others can be an important source of information. However, one needs to be careful here and make sure that all data gathering respects both local and international privacy regulations.

SAMPLING

The aim of sampling is to take a subset of past customer data and use that to build an analytical model. A first obvious question concerns the need for sampling. With the availability of high performance computing facilities (e.g., grid/cloud computing), one could also directly analyze the full data set. However, a key requirement for a good sample is that it should be representative of the future customers on which the analytical model will be run. Hence, the timing aspect becomes important because customers of today are more similar to customers of tomorrow than customers of yesterday. Choosing the optimal time window for the sample involves a trade-off between lots of data (and hence a more robust analytical model) and recent data (which may be more representative). The sample should also be taken from an average business period to get a picture of the target population that is as accurate as possible.

It speaks for itself that sampling bias should be avoided as much as possible. However, this is not always straightforward. Let's take the example of credit scoring. Assume one wants to build an application scorecard to score mortgage applications. The future population then consists of all customers who come to the bank and apply for a mortgage—the so-called through-the-door (TTD) population. One

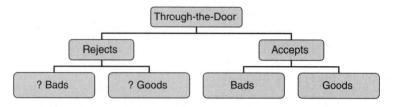

Figure 2.1 The Reject Inference Problem in Credit Scoring

then needs a subset of the historical TTD population to build an analytical model. However, in the past, the bank was already applying a credit policy (either expert based or based on a previous analytical model). This implies that the historical TTD population has two subsets: the customers that were accepted with the old policy, and the ones that were rejected (see Figure 2.1). Obviously, for the latter, we don't know the target value since they were never granted the credit. When building a sample, one can then only make use of those that were accepted, which clearly implies a bias. Procedures for reject inference have been suggested in the literature to deal with this sampling bias problem.[1] Unfortunately, all of these procedures make assumptions and none of them works perfectly. One of the most popular solutions is bureau-based inference, whereby a sample of past customers is given to the credit bureau to determine their target label (good or bad payer).

When thinking even closer about the target population for credit scoring, another forgotten subset are the withdrawals. These are the customers who were offered credit but decided not to take it (despite the fact that they may have been classified as good by the old scorecard). To be representative, these customers should also be included in the development sample. However, to the best of our knowledge, no procedures for withdrawal inference are typically applied in the industry.

In stratified sampling, a sample is taken according to predefined strata. Consider, for example, a churn prediction or fraud detection context in which data sets are typically very skewed (e.g., 99 percent nonchurners and 1 percent churners). When stratifying according to the target churn indicator, the sample will contain exactly the same percentages of churners and nonchurners as in the original data.

TYPES OF DATA ELEMENTS

It is important to appropriately consider the different types of data elements at the start of the analysis. The following types of data elements can be considered:

- Continuous: These are data elements that are defined on an interval that can be limited or unlimited. Examples include income, sales, RFM (recency, frequency, monetary).
- Categorical
  - Nominal: These are data elements that can only take on a limited set of values with no meaningful ordering in between. Examples include marital status, profession, purpose of loan.
  - Ordinal: These are data elements that can only take on a limited set of values with a meaningful ordering in between. Examples include credit rating; age coded as young, middle aged, and old.
  - Binary: These are data elements that can only take on two values. Examples include gender, employment status.

Appropriately distinguishing between these different data elements is of key importance to start the analysis when importing the data into an analytics tool. For example, if marital status were to be incorrectly specified as a continuous data element, then the software would calculate its mean, standard deviation, and so on, which is obviously meaningless.

VISUAL DATA EXPLORATION AND EXPLORATORY STATISTICAL ANALYSIS

Visual data exploration is a very important part of getting to know your data in an "informal" way. It allows you to get some initial insights into the data, which can then be usefully adopted throughout the modeling. Different plots/graphs can be useful here. A first popular example is pie charts. A pie chart represents a variable's distribution as a pie, whereby each section represents the portion of the total percent taken by each value of the variable. Figure 2.2 represents a pie chart for a housing variable for which one's status can be own, rent, or

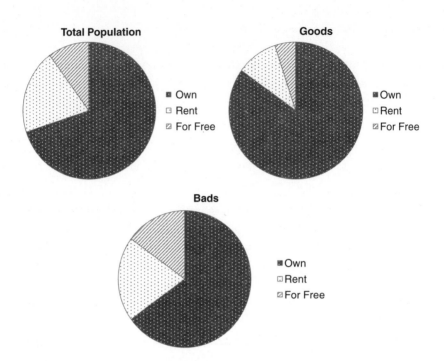

Figure 2.2   Pie Charts for Exploratory Data Analysis

for free (e.g., live with parents). By doing a separate pie chart analysis for the goods and bads, respectively, one can see that more goods own their residential property than bads, which can be a very useful starting insight. Bar charts represent the frequency of each of the values (either absolute or relative) as bars. Other handy visual tools are histograms and scatter plots. A histogram provides an easy way to visualize the central tendency and to determine the variability or spread of the data. It also allows you to contrast the observed data with standard known distributions (e.g., normal distribution). Scatter plots allow you to visualize one variable against another to see whether there are any correlation patterns in the data. Also, OLAP-based multidimensional data analysis can be usefully adopted to explore patterns in the data.

A next step after visual analysis could be inspecting some basic statistical measurements, such as averages, standard deviations, minimum, maximum, percentiles, and confidence intervals. One could calculate these measures separately for each of the target classes (e.g., good versus bad customer) to see whether there are any interesting patterns present (e.g., whether bad payers usually have a lower average age than good payers).

MISSING VALUES

Missing values can occur because of various reasons. The information can be nonapplicable. For example, when modeling time of churn, this information is only available for the churners and not for the nonchurners because it is not applicable there. The information can also be undisclosed. For example, a customer decided not to disclose his or her income because of privacy. Missing data can also originate because of an error during merging (e.g., typos in name or ID).

Some analytical techniques (e.g., decision trees) can directly deal with missing values. Other techniques need some additional preprocessing. The following are the most popular schemes to deal with missing values:[2]

- **Replace (impute).** This implies replacing the missing value with a known value (e.g., consider the example in Table 2.1). One could impute the missing credit bureau scores with the average or median of the known values. For marital status, the mode can then be used. One could also apply regression-based imputation whereby a regression model is estimated to model a target variable (e.g., credit bureau score) based on the other information available (e.g., age, income). The latter is more sophisticated, although the added value from an empirical viewpoint (e.g., in terms of model performance) is questionable.
- **Delete.** This is the most straightforward option and consists of deleting observations or variables with lots of missing values. This, of course, assumes that information is missing at random and has no meaningful interpretation and/or relationship to the target.
- **Keep.** Missing values can be meaningful (e.g., a customer did not disclose his or her income because he or she is currently unemployed). Obviously, this is clearly related to the target (e.g., good/bad risk or churn) and needs to be considered as a separate category.

Table 2.1 Dealing with Missing Values

ID	Age	Income	Marital Status	Credit Bureau Score	Class
1	34	1,800	?	620	Churner
2	28	1,200	Single	?	Nonchurner
3	22	1,000	Single	?	Nonchurner
4	60	2,200	Widowed	700	Churner
5	58	2,000	Married	?	Nonchurner
6	44	?	?	?	Nonchurner
7	22	1,200	Single	?	Nonchurner
8	26	1,500	Married	350	Nonchurner
9	34	?	Single	?	Churner
10	50	2,100	Divorced	?	Nonchurner

As a practical way of working, one can first start with statistically testing whether missing information is related to the target variable (using, for example, a chi-squared test, discussed later). If yes, then we can adopt the keep strategy and make a special category for it. If not, one can, depending on the number of observations available, decide to either delete or impute.

OUTLIER DETECTION AND TREATMENT

Outliers are extreme observations that are very dissimilar to the rest of the population. Actually, two types of outliers can be considered:

1. Valid observations (e.g., salary of boss is $1 million)
2. Invalid observations (e.g., age is 300 years)

Both are univariate outliers in the sense that they are outlying on one dimension. However, outliers can be hidden in unidimensional views of the data. Multivariate outliers are observations that are outlying in multiple dimensions. Figure 2.3 gives an example of two outlying observations considering both the dimensions of income and age.

Two important steps in dealing with outliers are detection and treatment. A first obvious check for outliers is to calculate the minimum and maximum values for each of the data elements. Various graphical

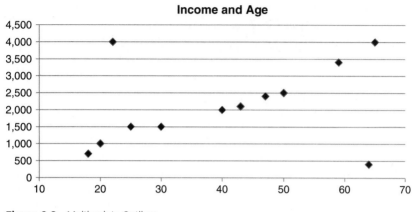

Figure 2.3 Multivariate Outliers

tools can be used to detect outliers. Histograms are a first example. Figure 2.4 presents an example of a distribution for age whereby the circled areas clearly represent outliers.

Another useful visual mechanism are box plots. A box plot represents three key quartiles of the data: the first quartile (25 percent of the observations have a lower value), the median (50 percent of the observations have a lower value), and the third quartile (75 percent of the observations have a lower value). All three quartiles are represented as a box. The minimum and maximum values are then also

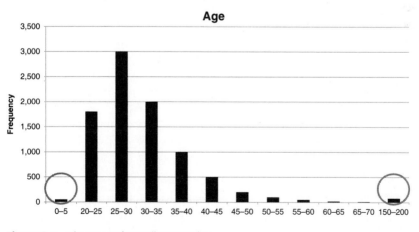

Figure 2.4 Histograms for Outlier Detection

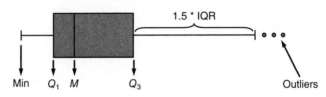

Figure 2.5 Box Plots for Outlier Detection

added unless they are too far away from the edges of the box. Too far away is then quantified as more than 1.5 * Interquartile Range (IQR = Q_3 – Q_1). Figure 2.5 gives an example of a box plot in which three outliers can be seen.

Another way is to calculate z-scores, measuring how many standard deviations an observation lies away from the mean, as follows:

$$z_i = \frac{x_i - \mu}{\sigma}$$

where μ represents the average of the variable and σ its standard deviation. An example is given in Table 2.2. Note that by definition, the z-scores will have 0 mean and unit standard deviation.

A practical rule of thumb then defines outliers when the absolute value of the z-score $|z|$ is bigger than 3. Note that the z-score relies on the normal distribution.

The above methods all focus on univariate outliers. Multivariate outliers can be detected by fitting regression lines and inspecting the

Table 2.2   Z-Scores for Outlier Detection

ID	Age	Z-Score
1	30	(30 – 40)/10 = –1
2	50	(50 – 40)/10 = +1
3	10	(10 – 40)/10 = –3
4	40	(40 – 40)/10 = 0
5	60	(60 – 40)/10 = +2
6	80	(80 – 40)/10 = +4
...	...	...
	$\mu = 40$ $\sigma = 10$	$\mu = 0$ $\sigma = 1$

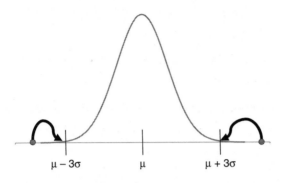

Figure 2.6 Using the Z-Scores for Truncation

observations with large errors (using, for example, a residual plot). Alternative methods are clustering or calculating the Mahalanobis distance. Note, however, that although potentially useful, multivariate outlier detection is typically not considered in many modeling exercises due to the typical marginal impact on model performance.

Some analytical techniques (e.g., decision trees, neural networks, Support Vector Machines (SVMs)) are fairly robust with respect to outliers. Others (e.g., linear/logistic regression) are more sensitive to them. Various schemes exist to deal with outliers. It highly depends on whether the outlier represents a valid or invalid observation. For invalid observations (e.g., age is 300 years), one could treat the outlier as a missing value using any of the schemes discussed in the previous section. For valid observations (e.g., income is $1 million), other schemes are needed. A popular scheme is truncation/capping/winsorizing. One hereby imposes both a lower and upper limit on a variable and any values below/above are brought back to these limits. The limits can be calculated using the z-scores (see Figure 2.6), or the IQR (which is more robust than the z-scores), as follows:

Upper/lower limit = $M \pm 3s$, with M = median and s = IQR/(2×0.6745).[3]

A sigmoid transformation ranging between 0 and 1 can also be used for capping, as follows:

$$f(x) = \frac{1}{1 + e^{-x}}$$

In addition, expert-based limits based on business knowledge and/ or experience can be imposed.

STANDARDIZING DATA

Standardizing data is a data preprocessing activity targeted at scaling variables to a similar range. Consider, for example, two variables: gender (coded as 0/1) and income (ranging between $0 and $1 million). When building logistic regression models using both information elements, the coefficient for income might become very small. Hence, it could make sense to bring them back to a similar scale. The following standardization procedures could be adopted:

- Min/max standardization

  - $X_{new} = \dfrac{X_{old} - \min(X_{old})}{\max(X_{old}) - \min(X_{old})}(newmax - newmin) + newmin,$

    whereby newmax and newmin are the newly imposed maximum and minimum (e.g., 1 and 0).
- Z-score standardization
  - Calculate the z-scores (see the previous section)
- Decimal scaling
  - Dividing by a power of 10 as follows: $X_{new} = \dfrac{X_{old}}{10^n}$, with n the number of digits of the maximum absolute value.

Again note that standardization is especially useful for regression-based approaches, but is not needed for decision trees, for example.

CATEGORIZATION

Categorization (also known as coarse classification, classing, grouping, binning, etc.) can be done for various reasons. For categorical variables, it is needed to reduce the number of categories. Consider, for example, the variable "purpose of loan" having 50 different values. When this variable would be put into a regression model, one would need 49 dummy variables (50 − 1 because of the collinearity), which would necessitate the estimation of 49 parameters for only one variable. With categorization, one would create categories of values such

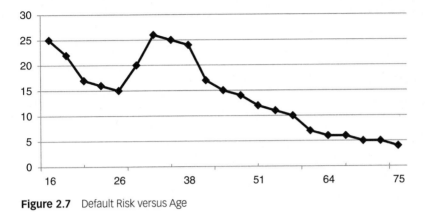

Figure 2.7 Default Risk versus Age

that fewer parameters will have to be estimated and a more robust model is obtained.

For continuous variables, categorization may also be very beneficial. Consider, for example, the age variable and its risk as depicted in Figure 2.7. Clearly, there is a nonmonotonous relation between risk and age. If a nonlinear model (e.g., neural network, support vector machine) were to be used, then the nonlinearity can be perfectly modeled. However, if a regression model were to be used (which is typically more common because of its interpretability), then since it can only fit a line, it will miss out on the nonmonotonicity. By categorizing the variable into ranges, part of the nonmonotonicity can be taken into account in the regression. Hence, categorization of continuous variables can be useful to model nonlinear effects into linear models.

Various methods can be used to do categorization. Two very basic methods are equal interval binning and equal frequency binning. Consider, for example, the income values 1,000, 1,200, 1,300, 2,000, 1,800, and 1,400. Equal interval binning would create two bins with the same range—Bin 1: 1,000, 1,500 and Bin 2: 1,500, 2,000—whereas equal frequency binning would create two bins with the same number of observations—Bin 1: 1,000, 1,200, 1,300; Bin 2: 1,400, 1,800, 2,000. However, both methods are quite basic and do not take into account a target variable (e.g., churn, fraud, credit risk).

Chi-squared analysis is a more sophisticated way to do coarse classification. Consider the example depicted in Table 2.3 for coarse classifying a residential status variable.

Table 2.3 Coarse Classifying the Residential Status Variable

Attribute	Owner	Rent Unfurnished	Rent Furnished	With Parents	Other	No Answer	Total
Goods	6,000	1,600	350	950	90	10	9,000
Bads	300	400	140	100	50	10	1,000
Good: bad odds	20:1	4:1	2.5:1	9.5:1	1.8:1	1:1	9:1

Source: L. C. Thomas, D. Edelman, and J. N. Crook, *Credit Scoring and its Applications* (Society for Industrial and Applied Mathematics, Philadelphia, Penn., 2002).

Suppose we want three categories and consider the following options:

- Option 1: owner, renters, others
- Option 2: owner, with parents, others

Both options can now be investigated using chi-squared analysis. The purpose is to compare the empirically observed with the independence frequencies. For option 1, the empirically observed frequencies are depicted in Table 2.4.

The independence frequencies can be calculated as follows. The number of good owners, given that the odds are the same as in the whole population, is 6,300/10,000 × 9,000/10,000 × 10,000 = 5,670. One then obtains Table 2.5.

The more the numbers in both tables differ, the less independence, hence better dependence and a better coarse classification. Formally, one can calculate the chi-squared distance as follows:

$$\chi^2 = \frac{(6000-5670)^2}{5670} + \frac{(300-630)^2}{630} + \frac{(1950-2241)^2}{2241} + \frac{(540-249)^2}{249}$$
$$+ \frac{(1050-1089)^2}{1089} + \frac{(160-121)^2}{121} = 583$$

Table 2.4 Empirical Frequencies Option 1 for Coarse Classifying Residential Status

Attribute	Owner	Renters	Others	Total
Goods	6,000	1,950	1,050	9,000
Bads	300	540	160	1,000
Total	6,300	2,490	1,210	10,000

Table 2.5 Independence Frequencies Option 1 for Coarse Classifying Residential Status

Attribute	Owner	Renters	Others	Total
Goods	5,670	2,241	1,089	9,000
Bads	630	249	121	1,000
Total	6,300	2,490	1,210	10,000

Likewise, for option 2, the calculation becomes:

$$\chi^2 = \frac{(6000-5670)^2}{5670} + \frac{(300-630)^2}{630} + \frac{(950-945)^2}{945} + \frac{(100-105)^2}{105}$$
$$+ \frac{(2050-2385)^2}{2385} + \frac{(600-265)^2}{265} = 662$$

So, based upon the chi-squared values, option 2 is the better categorization. Note that formally, one needs to compare the value with a chi-squared distribution with $k - 1$ degrees of freedom with k being the number of values of the characteristic.

Many analytics software tools have built-in facilities to do categorization using chi-squared analysis. A very handy and simple approach (available in Microsoft Excel) is pivot tables. Consider the example shown in Table 2.6.

One can then construct a pivot table and calculate the odds as shown in Table 2.7.

Table 2.6 Coarse Classifying the Purpose Variable

Customer ID	Age	Purpose	...	G/B
C1	44	Car		G
C2	20	Cash		G
C3	58	Travel		B
C4	26	Car		G
C5	30	Study		B
C6	32	House		G
C7	48	Cash		B
C8	60	Car		G
...	...	...		

Table 2.7 Pivot Table for Coarse Classifying the Purpose Variable

	Car	Cash	Travel	Study	House	...
Good	1,000	2,000	3,000	100	5,000	
Bad	500	100	200	80	800	
Odds	2	20	15	1.25	6.25	

We can then categorize the values based on similar odds. For example, category 1 (car, study), category 2 (house), and category 3 (cash, travel).

WEIGHTS OF EVIDENCE CODING

Categorization reduces the number of categories for categorical variables. For continuous variables, categorization will introduce new variables. Consider a regression model with age (4 categories, so 3 parameters) and purpose (5 categories, so 4 parameters) characteristics. The model then looks as follows:

$$Y = \beta_0 + \beta_1 Age_1 + \beta_2 Age_2 + \beta_3 Age_3 + \beta_4 Purp_1 + \beta_5 Purp_2 + \beta_6 Purp_3 + \beta_7 Purp_4$$

Despite having only two characteristics, the model still needs 8 parameters to be estimated. It would be handy to have a monotonic transformation $f(.)$ such that our model could be rewritten as follows:

$$Y = \beta_0 + \beta_1 f(Age_1, Age_2, Age_3) + \beta_2 f(Purp_1, Purp_2, Purp_3, Purp_4)$$

The transformation should have a monotonically increasing or decreasing relationship with Y. Weights-of-evidence coding is one example of a transformation that can be used for this purpose. This is illustrated in Table 2.8.

The WOE is calculated as: ln(Distr. Good/Distr. Bad). Because of the logarithmic transformation, a positive (negative) WOE means Distr. Good > (<) Distr. Bad. The WOE transformation thus implements a transformation monotonically related to the target variable.

The model can then be reformulated as follows:

$$Y = \beta_0 + \beta_1 WOE_{age} + \beta_2 WOE_{purpose}$$

Table 2.8 Calculating Weights of Evidence (WOE)

Age	Count	Distr. Count	Goods	Distr. Good	Bads	Distr. Bad	WOE
Missing	50	2.50%	42	2.33%	8	4.12%	−57.28%
18–22	200	10.00%	152	8.42%	48	24.74%	−107.83%
23–26	300	15.00%	246	13.62%	54	27.84%	−71.47%
27–29	450	22.50%	405	22.43%	45	23.20%	−3.38%
30–35	500	25.00%	475	26.30%	25	12.89%	71.34%
35–44	350	17.50%	339	18.77%	11	5.67%	119.71%
44+	150	7.50%	147	8.14%	3	1.55%	166.08%
	2,000		1,806		194		

This gives a more concise model than the model with which we started this section. However, note that the interpretability of the model becomes somewhat less straightforward when WOE variables are being used.

VARIABLE SELECTION

Many analytical modeling exercises start with tons of variables, of which typically only a few actually contribute to the prediction of the target variable. For example, the average application/behavioral scorecard in credit scoring has somewhere between 10 and 15 variables. The key question is how to find these variables. Filters are a very handy variable selection mechanism. They work by measuring univariate correlations between each variable and the target. As such, they allow for a quick screening of which variables should be retained for further analysis. Various filter measures have been suggested in the literature. One can categorize them as depicted in Table 2.9.

The Pearson correlation ρ_P is calculated as follows:

$$\rho_P = \frac{\sum_{i=1}^{n}(X_i - \bar{X})(Y_i - \bar{Y})}{\sqrt{\sum_{i=1}^{n}(X_i - \bar{X})^2}\sqrt{\sum_{i=1}^{n}(Y_i - \bar{Y})^2}}$$

It measures a linear dependency between two variables and always varies between −1 and +1. To apply it as a filter, one could select all variables for which the Pearson correlation is significantly different

Table 2.9 Filters for Variable Selection

	Continuous Target (e.g., CLV, LGD)	Categorical Target (e.g., churn, fraud, credit risk)
Continuous variable	Pearson correlation	Fisher score
Categorical variable	Fisher score/ANOVA	Information value (IV) Cramer's V Gain/entropy

from 0 (according to the *p*-value), or, for example, the ones where $|\rho_P| > 0.50$.

The Fisher score can be calculated as follows:

$$\frac{\left|\overline{X}_G - \overline{X}_B\right|}{\sqrt{s_G^2 + s_B^2}},$$

where $\overline{X}_G$ ($\overline{X}_B$) represents the average value of the variable for the Goods (Bads) and s_G^2 (s_B^2) the corresponding variances. High values of the Fisher score indicate a predictive variable. To apply it as a filter, one could, for example, keep the top 10 percent. Note that the Fisher score may generalize to a well-known analysis of variance (ANOVA) in case a variable has multiple categories.

The information value (IV) filter is based on weights of evidence and is calculated as follows:

$$IV = \sum_{i=1}^{k}(Dist\ Good_i - Dist\ Bad_i) * WOE_i$$

where k represents the number of categories of the variable. For the example discussed in Table 2.8, the calculation becomes as depicted in Table 2.10.

The following rules of thumb apply for the information value:

- ■ < 0.02: unpredictive
- ■ 0.02–0.1: weak predictive
- ■ 0.1–0.3: medium predictive
- ■ > 0.3: strong predictive

Note that the information value assumes that the variable has been categorized. It can actually also be used to adjust/steer the categorization so as to optimize the IV. Many software tools will provide

Table 2.10 Calculating the Information Value Filter Measure

Age	Count	Distr. Count	Goods	Distr. Good	Bads	Distr. Bad	WOE	IV
Missing	50	2.50%	42	2.33%	8	4.12%	−57.28%	0.0103
18–22	200	10.00%	152	8.42%	48	24.74%	−107.83%	0.1760
23–26	300	15.00%	246	13.62%	54	27.84%	−71.47%	0.1016
27–29	450	22.50%	405	22.43%	45	23.20%	−3.38%	0.0003
30–35	500	25.00%	475	26.30%	25	12.89%	71.34%	0.0957
35–44	350	17.50%	339	18.77%	11	5.67%	119.71%	0.1568
44+	150	7.50%	147	8.14%	3	1.55%	166.08%	0.1095
Information Value								**0.6502**

interactive support to do this, whereby the modeler can adjust the categories and gauge the impact on the IV. To apply it as a filter, one can calculate the information value of all (categorical) variables and only keep those for which the IV > 0.1 or, for example, the top 10%.

Another filter measure based upon chi-squared analysis is Cramer's V. Consider the contingency table depicted in Table 2.11 for marital status versus good/bad.

Similar to the example discussed in the section on categorization, the chi-squared value for independence can then be calculated as follows:

$$\chi^2 = \frac{(500-480)^2}{480} + \frac{(100-120)^2}{120} + \frac{(300-320)^2}{320} + \frac{(100-80)^2}{80} = 10.41$$

This follows a chi-squared distribution with $k - 1$ degrees of freedom, with k being the number of classes of the characteristic. The Cramer's V measure can then be calculated as follows:

$$Cramer's\ V = \sqrt{\frac{\chi^2}{n}} = 0.10,$$

Table 2.11 Contingency Table for Marital Status versus Good/Bad Customer

	Good	Bad	Total
Married	500	100	600
Not Married	300	100	400
Total	800	200	1,000

with n being the number of observations in the data set. Cramer's V is always bounded between 0 and 1 and higher values indicate better predictive power. As a rule of thumb, a cutoff of 0.1 is commonly adopted. One can then again select all variables where Cramer's V is bigger than 0.1, or consider the top 10 percent. Note that the information value and Cramer's V typically consider the same characteristics as most important.

Filters are very handy because they allow you to reduce the number of dimensions of the data set early in the analysis in a quick way. Their main drawback is that they work univariately and typically do not consider, for example, correlation between the dimensions individually. Hence, a follow-up input selection step during the modeling phase will be necessary to further refine the characteristics. Also worth mentioning here is that other criteria may play a role in selecting variables. For example, from a regulatory compliance viewpoint, some variables may not be used in analytical models (e.g., the U.S. Equal Credit Opportunities Act states that one cannot discriminate credit based on age, gender, marital status, ethnic origin, religion, and so on, so these variables should be left out of the analysis as soon as possible). Note that different regulations may apply in different geographical regions and hence should be checked. Also, operational issues could be considered (e.g., trend variables could be very predictive but may require too much time to be computed in a real-time online scoring environment).

SEGMENTATION

Sometimes the data is segmented before the analytical modeling starts. A first reason for this could be strategic (e.g., banks might want to adopt special strategies to specific segments of customers). It could also be motivated from an operational viewpoint (e.g., new customers must have separate models because the characteristics in the standard model do not make sense operationally for them). Segmentation could also be needed to take into account significant variable interactions (e.g., if one variable strongly interacts with a number of others, it might be sensible to segment according to this variable).

The segmentation can be conducted using the experience and knowledge from a business expert, or it could be based on statistical analysis using, for example, decision trees (see Chapter 3), k-means, or self-organizing maps (see Chapter 4).

Segmentation is a very useful preprocessing activity because one can now estimate different analytical models each tailored to a specific segment. However, one needs to be careful with it because by segmenting, the number of analytical models to estimate will increase, which will obviously also increase the production, monitoring, and maintenance costs.

NOTES

1. J. Banasik, J. N. Crook, and L. C. Thomas, "Sample Selection Bias in Credit Scoring Models" in *Proceedings of the Seventh Conference on Credit Scoring and Credit Control* (Edinburgh University, 2001).
2. R. J. A. Little and D. B. Rubin, *Statistical Analysis with Missing Data* (Wiley-Interscience, Hoboken, New Jersey, 2002).
3. T. Van Gestel and B. Baesens, *Credit Risk Management: Basic Concepts: Financial Risk Components, Rating Analysis, Models, Economic and Regulatory Capital*, Oxford University Press, Oxford, England, ISBN 978-0-19-954511-7, 2009.

CHAPTER **3**

Predictive
Analytics

I n predictive analytics, the aim is to build an analytical model predicting a target measure of interest.[1] The target is then typically used to steer the learning process during an optimization procedure. Two types of predictive analytics can be distinguished: regression and classification. In regression, the target variable is continuous. Popular examples are predicting stock prices, loss given default (LGD), and customer lifetime value (CLV). In classification, the target is categorical. It can be binary (e.g., fraud, churn, credit risk) or multiclass (e.g., predicting credit ratings). Different types of predictive analytics techniques have been suggested in the literature. In what follows, we will discuss a selection of techniques with a particular focus on the practitioner's perspective.

TARGET DEFINITION

Because the target variable plays an important role in the learning process, it is of key importance that it is appropriately defined. In what follows, we will give some examples.

In a customer attrition setting, churn can be defined in various ways. Active churn implies that the customer stops the relationship with the firm. In a contractual setting (e.g., postpaid telco), this can be easily detected when the customer cancels the contract. In a noncontractual setting (e.g., supermarket), this is less obvious and needs to be operationalized in a specific way. For example, a customer churns if he or she has not purchased any products during the previous three months. Passive churn occurs when a customer decreases the intensity of the relationship with the firm, for example, by decreasing product or service usage. Forced churn implies that the company stops the relationship with the customer because he or she has been engaged in fraudulent activities. Expected churn occurs when the customer no longer needs the product or service (e.g., baby products).

In credit scoring, a defaulter can be defined in various ways. For example, according to the Basel II/Basel III regulation, a defaulter is defined as someone who is 90 days in payment arrears. In the United States, this has been changed to 180 days for mortgages and qualifying revolving exposures, and 120 days for other retail exposures. Other countries (e.g., the United Kingdom) have made similar adjustments.

In fraud detection, the target fraud indicator is usually hard to determine because one can never be fully sure that a certain transaction (e.g., credit card) or claim (e.g., insurance) is fraudulent. Typically, the decision is then made based on a legal judgment or a high suspicion by a business expert.[2]

In response modeling, the response target can be defined in various ways. *Gross response* refers to the customers who purchase after having received the marketing message. However, it is more interesting to define the target as the *net response,* being the customers who purchase because of having received the marketing message, the so-called swingers.

Customer lifetime value (CLV) is a continuous target variable and is usually defined as follows:[3]

$$CLV = \sum_{i=1}^{n} \frac{(R_t - C_t)s_t}{(1+d)^t}$$

where n represents the time horizon considered (typically two to three years), R_t the revenue at time t (both direct and indirect), C_t the costs incurred at time t (both direct and indirect), s_t the survival probability

Table 3.1 Example CLV Calculation

Month t	Revenue in Month t (R_t)	Cost in Month t (C_t)	Survival Probability in Month t (s_t)	$(R_t - C_t) * s_t / (1 + d)^t$
1	150	5	0.94	135.22
2	100	10	0.92	82.80
3	120	5	0.88	101.20
4	100	0	0.84	84.00
5	130	10	0.82	98.40
6	140	5	0.74	99.90
7	80	15	0.7	45.50
8	100	10	0.68	61.20
9	120	10	0.66	72.60
10	90	20	0.6	42.00
11	100	0	0.55	55.00
12	130	10	0.5	60.00
			CLV	**937.82**
	Yearly WACC	**10%**		
	Monthly WACC	**1%**		

at time t (see Chapter 5), and d the discounting factor (typically the weighted average cost of capital [WACC]). Defining all these parameters is by no means a trivial exercise and should be done in close collaboration with the business expert. Table 3.1 gives an example of calculating CLV.

Loss given default (LGD) is an important credit risk parameter in a Basel II/Basel III setting.[4] It represents the percentage of the exposure likely to be lost upon default. Again, when defining it, one needs to decide on the time horizon (typically two to three years), what costs to include (both direct and indirect), and what discount factor to adopt (typically the contract rate).

Before starting the analytical step, it is really important to check the robustness and stability of the target definition. In credit scoring, one commonly adopts roll rate analysis for this purpose as illustrated in Figure 3.1. The purpose here is to visualize how customers move from one delinquency state to another during a specific time frame. It

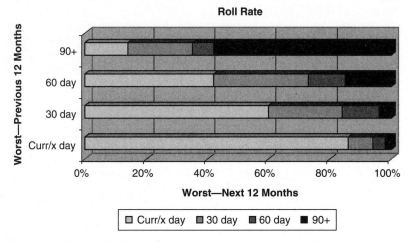

Figure 3.1 Roll Rate Analysis
Source: N. Siddiqi, *Credit Risk Scorecards: Developing and Implementing Intelligent Credit Scoring* (Hoboken, NJ: John Wiley & Sons, 2005).

can be easily seen from the plot that once the customer has reached 90 or more days of payment arrears, he or she is unlikely to recover.

LINEAR REGRESSION

Linear regression is a baseline modeling technique to model a continuous target variable. For example, in a CLV modeling context, a linear regression model can be defined to model CLV in terms of the RFM (recency, frequency, monetary value) predictors as follows:

$$CLV = \beta_0 + \beta_1 R + \beta_2 F + \beta_3 M$$

The β parameters are then typically estimated using ordinary least squares (OLS) to minimize the sum of squared errors. As part of the estimation, one then also obtains standard errors, p-values indicating variable importance (remember important variables get low p-values), and confidence intervals. A key advantage of linear regression is that it is simple and usually works very well.

Note that more sophisticated variants have been suggested in the literature (e.g., ridge regression, lasso regression, time series models [ARIMA, VAR, GARCH], multivariate adaptive regression splines [MARS]).

LOGISTIC REGRESSION

Consider a classification data set for response modeling as depicted in Table 3.2.

When modeling the response using linear regression, one gets:

$$Y = \beta_0 + \beta_1 \text{Age} + \beta_2 \text{Income} + \beta_3 \text{Gender}$$

When estimating this using OLS, two key problems arise:

1. The errors/target are not normally distributed but follow a Bernoulli distribution.
2. There is no guarantee that the target is between 0 and 1, which would be handy because it can then be interpreted as a probability.

Consider now the following bounding function:

$$f(z) = \frac{1}{1 + e^{-z}}$$

which can be seen in Figure 3.2.

For every possible value of z, the outcome is always between 0 and 1. Hence, by combining the linear regression with the bounding function, we get the following logistic regression model:

$$P(response = yes|age, income, gender) = \frac{1}{1 + e^{-(\beta_0 + \beta_1 age + \beta_2 income + \beta_3 gender)}}$$

The outcome of the above model is always bounded between 0 and 1, no matter what values of age, income, and gender are being used, and can as such be interpreted as a probability.

Table 3.2 Example Classification Data Set

Customer	Age	Income	Gender	...	Response	Y
John	30	1,200	M		No	0
Sarah	25	800	F		Yes	1
Sophie	52	2,200	F		Yes	1
David	48	2,000	M		No	0
Peter	34	1,800	M		Yes	1

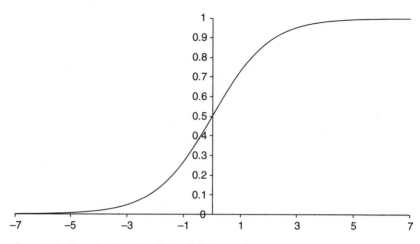

Figure 3.2 Bounding Function for Logistic Regression

The general formulation of the logistic regression model then becomes:

$$P(Y = 1 | X_1, \ldots, X_n) = \frac{1}{1 + e^{-(\beta_0 + \beta_1 X_1 + \cdots + \beta_N X_N)}},$$

or, alternately,

$$P(Y = 0 | X_1, \ldots, X_N) = 1 - P(Y = 1 | X_1, \ldots, X_N)$$

$$= 1 - \frac{1}{1 + e^{-(\beta_0 + \beta_1 X_1 + \cdots + \beta_N X_N)}} = \frac{1}{1 + e^{(\beta_0 + \beta_1 X_1 + \cdots + \beta_N X_i)}}$$

Hence, both $P(Y = 1 | X_1, \ldots, X_N)$ and $P(Y = 0 | X_1, \ldots, X_N)$ are bounded between 0 and 1.

Reformulating in terms of the odds, the model becomes:

$$\frac{P(Y = 1 | X_1, \ldots, X_N)}{P(Y = 0 | X_1, \ldots, X_N)} = e^{(\beta_0 + \beta_1 X_1 + \cdots + \beta_N X_N)}$$

or, in terms of log odds (logit),

$$\ln\left(\frac{P(Y = 1 | X_1, \ldots, X_N)}{P(Y = 0 | X_1, \ldots, X_N)}\right) = \beta_0 + \beta_1 X_1 + \cdots + \beta_N X_N$$

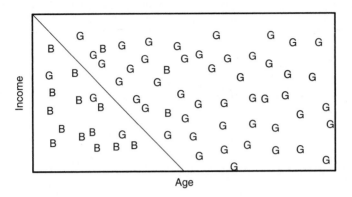

Figure 3.3 Decision Boundary of Logistic Regression

The β_i parameters of a logistic regression model are then estimated by optimizing a maximum likelihood function. Just as with linear regression, the optimization comes with standard errors, p-values for variable screening and confidence intervals.

Since logistic regression is linear in the log odds (logit), it basically estimates a linear decision boundary to separate both classes. This is illustrated in Figure 3.3.

To interpret a logistic regression model, one can calculate the odds ratio. Suppose variable X_i increases with one unit with all other variables being kept constant (*ceteris paribus*), then the new logit becomes the old logit with β_i added. Likewise, the new odds become the old odds multiplied by $e^{\beta i}$. The latter represents the odds ratio, that is, the multiplicative increase in the odds when X_i increases by 1 (*ceteris paribus*). Hence,

- $\beta_i > 0$ implies $e^{\beta i} > 1$ and the odds and probability increase with X_i
- $\beta_i < 0$ implies $e^{\beta i} < 1$ and the odds and probability decrease with X_i

Another way of interpreting a logistic regression model is by calculating the doubling amount. This represents the amount of change required for doubling the primary outcome odds. It can be easily seen that for a particular variable X_i, the doubling amount equals $\log(2)/\beta_i$.

Note that next to the $f(z)$ transformation discussed above, other transformations also have been suggested in the literature. Popular examples are the probit and cloglog transformation as follows:

$$f(z) = \frac{1}{\sqrt{2\pi}} \int_{-\infty}^{z} e^{\frac{-t^2}{2}} dt$$

$$f(z) = 1 - e^{-e^z}$$

The probit transformation was used in Moody's RiskCalc tool for predicting probability of default for firms.[5] Note, however, that empirical evidence suggests that all three transformations typically perform equally well.

DECISION TREES

Decision trees are recursive partitioning algorithms (RPAs) that come up with a tree-like structure representing patterns in an underlying data set.[6] Figure 3.4 provides an example of a decision tree.

The top node is the root node specifying a testing condition of which the outcome corresponds to a branch leading up to an internal node. The terminal nodes of the tree assign the classifications and are also referred to as the *leaf nodes*. Many algorithms have been suggested to construct decision trees. Amongst the most popular are: C4.5 (See5),[7] CART,[8] and CHAID.[9] These algorithms differ in their way of answering the key decisions to build a tree, which are:

- Splitting decision: Which variable to split at what value (e.g., age < 30 or not, income < 1,000 or not; marital status = married or not)
- Stopping decision: When to stop growing a tree?
- Assignment decision: What class (e.g., good or bad customer) to assign to a leaf node?

Usually, the assignment decision is the most straightforward to make since one typically looks at the majority class within the leaf node to make the decision. The other two decisions to be made are less straightforward and are elaborated on in what follows.

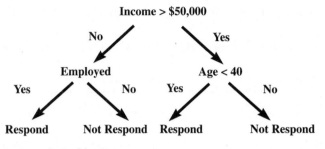

Figure 3.4 Example Decision Tree

In order to answer the splitting decision, one needs to define the concept of impurity or chaos. Consider, for example, the three data sets of Figure 3.5, each of which contains good (unfilled circles) and bad (filled circles) customers. Minimal impurity occurs when all customers are either good or bad. Maximal impurity occurs when one has the same number of good and bad customers (i.e., the data set in the middle).

Decision trees will now aim at minimizing the impurity in the data. In order to do so appropriately, one needs a measure to quantify impurity. Various measures have been introduced in the literature, and the most popular are:

- Entropy: $E(S) = -p_G \log_2(p_G) - p_B \log_2(p_B)$ (C4.5/See5)
- Gini: $Gini(S) = 2p_G p_B$ (CART)
- Chi-squared analysis (CHAID)

with p_G (p_B) being the proportions of good and bad, respectively. Both measures are depicted in Figure 3.6, where it can be clearly seen that the entropy (Gini) is minimal when all customers are either good or bad, and maximal in the case of the same number of good and bad customers.

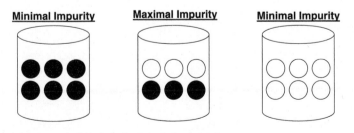

Figure 3.5 Example Data Sets for Calculating Impurity

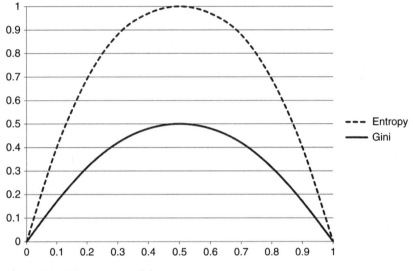

Figure 3.6 Entropy versus Gini

In answering the splitting decision, various candidate splits will now be evaluated in terms of their decrease in impurity. Consider, for example, a split on age as depicted in Figure 3.7.

The original data set had maximum entropy. The entropy calculations become:

- Entropy top node = $-1/2 \times \log_2(1/2) - 1/2 \times \log_2(1/2) = 1$
- Entropy left node = $-1/3 \times \log_2(1/3) - 2/3 \times \log_2(2/3) = 0.91$
- Entropy right node = $-1 \times \log_2(1) - 0 \times \log_2(0) = 0$

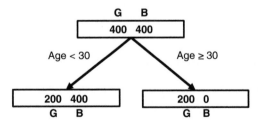

Figure 3.7 Calculating the Entropy for Age Split

The weighted decrease in entropy, also known as the *gain,* can then be calculated as follows:

$$Gain = 1 - (600/800) \times 0.91 - (200/800) \times 0 = 0.32$$

It speaks for itself that a larger gain is to be preferred. The decision tree algorithm will now consider different candidate splits for its root node and adopt a greedy strategy by picking the one with the biggest gain. Once the root node has been decided on, the procedure continues in a recursive way to continue tree growing.

The third decision relates to the stopping criterion. Obviously, if the tree continues to split, it will become very detailed with leaf nodes containing only a few observations. In other words, the tree will start to fit the specificities or noise in the data, which is also referred to as *overfitting.* In order to avoid this, the data will be split into a training sample and a validation sample. The training sample will be used to make the splitting decision. The validation sample is an independent sample, set aside to monitor the misclassification error (or any other performance metric). One then typically observes a pattern as depicted in Figure 3.8.

The error on the training sample keeps on decreasing as the splits become more and more specific toward it. On the validation sample, the error will initially decrease, but at some point it will increase back again since the splits become too specific for the training sample as the tree starts to memorize it. Where the validation set curve reaches its minimum, the procedure should be stopped or overfitting will occur. Note that besides classification error, one might also use accuracy or

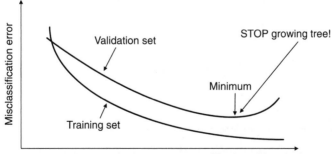

Figure 3.8 Using a Validation Set to Stop Growing a Decision Tree

profit based measures on the Y-axis to make the stopping decision. Also note that, sometimes, simplicity is preferred above accuracy, and one can select a tree that does not necessarily have minimum valida- tion set error, but a lower number of nodes.

In the example of Figure 3.4, every node had only two branches. The advantage of this is that the testing condition can be implemented as a simple yes/no question. Multiway splits allow for more than two branches and can provide trees that are wider but less deep. In a read once decision tree, a particular attribute can be used only once in a certain tree path. Every tree can also be represented as a rule set since every path from a root node to a leaf node makes up a simple if/then rule. These rules can then be easily implemented in all kinds of soft- ware packages (e.g., Microsoft Excel).

Decision trees essentially model decision boundaries orthogonal to the axes. This is illustrated in Figure 3.9 for an example decision tree.

Decision trees can also be used for continuous targets. Consider the example in Figure 3.10 of a regression tree for predicting LGD.

Other criteria need now be used to make the splitting decision because the impurity will need to be measured in another way. One way to measure impurity in a node is by calculating the mean squared error (MSE) as follows:

$$\frac{1}{n}\sum_{i=1}^{n}(Y_i - \bar{Y})^2,$$

where n represents the number of observations in a leave node, Y_i the value of observation i, and $\bar{Y}$, the average of all values in the leaf node.

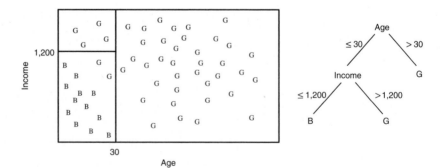

Figure 3.9 Decision Boundary of a Decision Tree

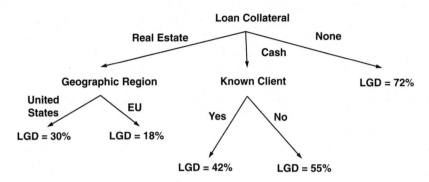

Figure 3.10 Example Regression Tree for Predicting LGD

Another way is by conducting a simple analysis of variance (ANOVA) test and calculate an F-statistic as follows:

$$F = \frac{SS_{between} / (B-1)}{SS_{within} / (n-B)} \sim F_{n-B,B-1},$$

whereby

$$SS_{between} = \sum_{b=1}^{B} n_b (\bar{Y}_b - \bar{Y})^2$$

$$SS_{within} = \sum_{b=1}^{B} \sum_{i=1}^{n_b} (Y_{bi} - \bar{Y}_b)^2$$

with B being the number of branches of the split, n_b the number of observations in branch b, $\bar{Y}_b$ the average in branch b, Y_{bi} the value of observation i in branch b, and $\bar{Y}$ the overall average. Good splits will then result in a high F value, or low corresponding p-value.

The stopping decision can be made in a similar way as for classification trees, but using a regression-based performance measure (e.g., mean squared error, mean absolute deviation, R-squared) on the Y-axis. The assignment decision can be made by assigning the mean (or median) to each leaf node. Note also that confidence intervals may be computed for each of the leaf nodes.

Decision trees can be used for various purposes in analytics. First, they can be used for input selection because attributes that occur at the top of the tree are more predictive of the target. One could also simply calculate the gain of a characteristic to gauge its predictive power.

Next, they can also be used for initial segmentation. One then typically builds a tree of two or three levels deep as the segmentation scheme and then uses second stage logistic regression models for further refinement. Finally, decision trees can also be used as the final analytical model to be used directly into production. A key advantage here is that the decision tree gives a white box model with a clear explanation behind how it reaches its classifications. Many software tools will also allow you to grow trees interactively by providing a splitting option at each level of the tree (e.g., a top five, or more, of splits amongst which the modeler can choose). This allows us to choose splits not only based upon impurity reduction, but also on the interpretability and/or computational complexity of the split criterion.

NEURAL NETWORKS

A first perspective on the origin of neural networks states that they are mathematical representations inspired by the functioning of the human brain. Another more realistic perspective sees neural networks as generalizations of existing statistical models. Let's take logistic regression as an example:

$$P(Y = 1 | X_1, \ldots, X_N) = \frac{1}{1 + e^{-(\beta_0 + \beta_1 X_1 + \cdots + \beta_N X_N)}},$$

This model can be seen in Figure 3.11.

The processing element or neuron in the middle basically performs two operations: it takes the inputs and multiplies them with the weights (including the intercept term β_0, which is called the *bias term*

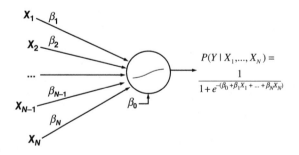

Figure 3.11 Neural Network Representation of Logistic Regression

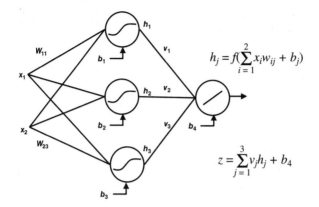

$$h_j = f(\sum_{i=1}^{2} x_i w_{ij} + b_j)$$

$$z = \sum_{j=1}^{3} v_j h_j + b_4$$

Figure 3.12 A Multilayer Perceptron (MLP) Neural Network

in neural networks) and then puts this into a nonlinear transformation function similar to the one we discussed in the section on logistic regression. So, logistic regression is a neural network with one neuron. Similarly, we could visualize linear regression as a one neuron neural network with the identity transformation $f(z) = z$. We can now generalize the above picture to a multilayer perceptron (MLP) neural network by adding more layers and neurons as shown in Figure 3.12.[10]

The example in Figure 3.12 is an MLP with one input layer, one hidden layer, and one output layer. The hidden layer has a nonlinear transformation function $f(\cdot)$ and the output layer a linear transformation function. The most popular transformation functions (also called squashing, activation functions) are:

■ Logistic, $f(z) = \dfrac{1}{1 + e^{-z}}$, ranging between 0 and 1

■ Hyperbolic tangent, $f(z) = \dfrac{e^z - e^{-z}}{e^z + e^{-z}}$, ranging between −1 and +1

■ Linear, $f(z) = z$, ranging between −∞ and +∞

For classification (e.g., churn, response, fraud), it is common practice to adopt a logistic transformation in the output layer, since the outputs can then be interpreted as probabilities.[11] For regression targets (e.g., CLV, LGD), one could use any of the transformation functions listed above. Typically, one will use hyperbolic tangent activation functions in the hidden layer.

In terms of hidden layers, theoretical works have shown that neural networks with one hidden layer are universal approximators, capable of approximating any function to any desired degree of accuracy on a compact interval.[12] Only for discontinuous functions (e.g., a saw tooth pattern), it could make sense to try out more hidden layers, although these patterns rarely occur in real-life data sets.

For simple statistical models (e.g., linear regression), there exists a closed-form mathematical formula for the optimal parameter values. However, for neural networks, the optimization is a lot more complex and the weights sitting on the connections need to be estimated using an iterative algorithm. The algorithm then optimizes a cost function, which may be similar to linear regression (mean squared error) or logistic regression (maximum likelihood based). The procedure typically starts from a set of random weights that are then iteratively adjusted to the patterns in the data using an optimization algorithm. Popular optimization algorithms here are backpropagation learning, conjugate gradient, and Levenberg-Marquardt.[13] A key issue to note here is the curvature of the objective function, which is not convex and may be multimodal as illustrated in Figure 3.13. The error function can thus have multiple local minima but typically only one global minimum. Hence, if the starting weights are chosen in a suboptimal way, one may get stuck in a local minimum. One way to deal with this is to try out different starting weights, start the optimization procedure for a few steps, and then continue with the best intermediate solution. The optimization procedure then continues until the error function shows no further progress, the weights stop changing substantially, or after a fixed number of optimization steps (also called *epochs*).

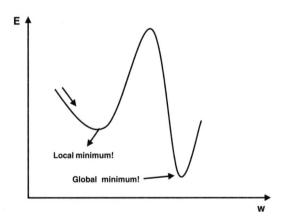

Figure 3.13 Local versus Global Minima

Although multiple output neurons could be used (predicting, for example, churn and CLV simultaneously), it is highly advised to use only one. The hidden neurons, however, should be carefully tuned and depend on the nonlinearity in the data. More complex, nonlinear patterns will require more hidden neurons. Although various procedures (e.g., cascade correlation, genetic algorithms, Bayesian methods) have been suggested in the scientific literature to do this, the most straightforward yet efficient procedure is as follows:[14]

- Split the data into a training, validation, and test set.
- Vary the number of hidden neurons from 1 to 10 in steps of 1 or more.
- Train a neural network on the training set and measure the performance on the validation set (may be train multiple neural networks to deal with the local minimum issue).
- Choose the number of hidden neurons with optimal validation set performance.
- Measure the performance on the independent test set.

Neural networks can model very complex patterns and decision boundaries in the data and, as such, are very powerful. In fact, they are so powerful that they can even model the noise in the training data, which is something that definitely should be avoided. One way to avoid this overfitting is by using a validation set in a similar way as with decision trees. This is illustrated in Figure 3.14. The training set is used here to estimate the weights and the validation set is again an independent data set used to decide when to stop training. Another scheme to prevent a neural network from overfitting is weight regularization, whereby the idea is to keep the weights small in absolute

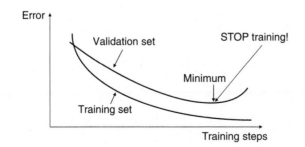

Figure 3.14 Using a Validation Set for Stopping Neural Network Training

sense because otherwise they may be fitting the noise in the data. This is then implemented by adding a weight size term (e.g., Euclidean norm) to the objective function of the neural network.[15]

Although neural networks have their merits in terms of modeling power, they are commonly described as black box techniques because they relate the inputs to the outputs in a mathematically complex, nontransparent, and opaque way. In application areas where interpretability may not be required (e.g., fraud detection, response modeling), they can be very successfully adopted as high-performance analytical tools.

However, in application areas where explanation is important (e.g., credit risk, medical diagnosis), one needs to be careful with neural networks because insight and comprehensibility in the underlying patterns is crucial.[16] Two ways to open up the neural network black box are rule extraction and two-stage models.

The purpose of rule extraction is to extract if/then classification rules mimicking the behavior of the neural network.[17] Two important approaches here are decompositional and pedagogical techniques. Decompositional rule extraction approaches decompose the network's internal workings by inspecting weights and/or activation values. A typical five-step approach here could be:[18]

1. Train a neural network and prune it as much as possible in terms of connections.
2. Categorize the hidden unit activation values using clustering.
3. Extract rules that describe the network outputs in terms of the categorized hidden unit activation values.
4. Extract rules that describe the categorized hidden unit activation values in terms of the network inputs.
5. Merge the rules obtained in steps 3 and 4 to directly relate the inputs to the outputs.

This is illustrated in Figure 3.15.

Note that steps 3 and 4 can be done simultaneously by building a decision tree relating the network outputs to the hidden unit activation values. Figure 3.16 gives an example of applying a decompositional neural network rule extraction approach in a credit scoring setting.

Step 1: Start from original data.

Customer	Age	Income	Gender	...	Response
Emma	28	1,000	F		No
Will	44	1,500	M		Yes
Dan	30	1,200	M		No
Bob	58	2,400	M		Yes

Step 2: Build a neural network (e.g. 3 hidden neurons).

Customer	Age	Income	Gender	h1	h2	h3	h1	h2	h3	Response
Emma	28	1,000	F	-1.20	2.34	0.66	1	3	2	No
Will	44	1,500	M	0.78	1.22	0.82	2	3	2	Yes
Dan	30	1,200	M	2.1	-0.18	0.16	3	1	2	No
Bob	58	2,400	M	-0.1	0.8	-2.34	1	2	1	Yes

Step 3: Categorize hidden unit activations.

If h1 = 1 and h2 = 3, then response = No
If h2 = 2, then response = Yes

Step 4: Extract rules relating network outputs to categorized hidden units.

If age < 28 and income < 1,000, then h1 = 1
If gender = F, then h2 = 3
If age > 34 and income > 1,500, then h2 = 2

Step 5: Extract rules relating categorized hidden units to inputs.

If age < 28 and income < 1,000 and gender = F then response = No
If age > 34 and income > 1,500 then response = Yes

Step 6: Merge both rule sets

Figure 3.15 Decompositional Approach for Neural Network Rule Extraction

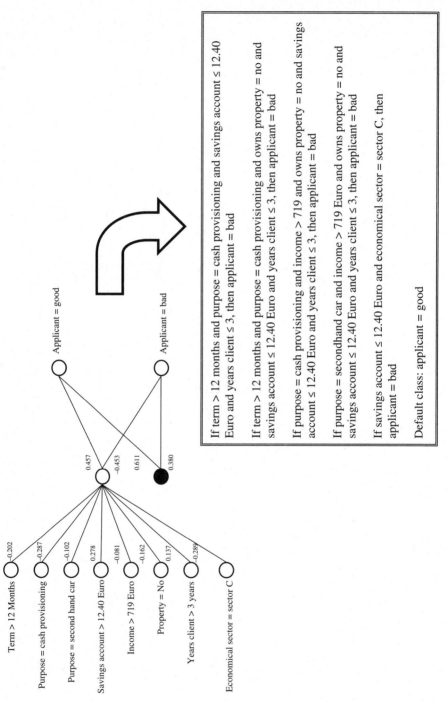

Figure 3.16 Example of Decompositional Neural Network Rule Extraction

54

Pedagogical rule extraction techniques consider the neural network as a black box and use the neural network predictions as input to a white box analytical technique such as decision trees.[19] This is illustrated in Figure 3.17.

In this approach, the learning data set can be further augmented with artificial data, which is then labeled (e.g., classified or predicted) by the neural network, so as to further increase the number of observations to make the splitting decisions when building the decision tree.

When using either decompositional or pedagogical rule extraction approaches, the rule sets should be evaluated in terms of their accuracy, conciseness (e.g., number of rules, number of conditions per rule), and fidelity. The latter measures to what extent the extracted rule set perfectly mimics the neural network and is calculated as follows:

		Neural Network Classification	
Rule set classification		Good	Bad
	Good	a	b
	Bad	c	d

Fidelity $= (a + d)/(b + c)$.

It is also important to always benchmark the extracted rules/trees with a tree built directly on the original data to see the benefit of going through the neural network.

Another approach to make neural networks more interpretable is by using a two-stage model setup.[20] The idea here is to estimate an easy to understand model first (e.g., linear regression, logistic regression). This will give us the interpretability part. In a second stage, a neural network is used to predict the errors made by the simple model using the same set of predictors. Both models are then combined in an additive way, for example, as follows:

- Target = linear regression $(X_1, X_2, \ldots X_N)$ + neural network $(X_1, X_2, \ldots X_N)$
- Score = logistic regression $(X_1, X_2, \ldots X_N)$ + neural network $(X_1, X_2, \ldots X_N)$

This setup provides an ideal balance between model interpretability (which comes from the first part) and model performance (which comes from the second part). This is illustrated in Figure 3.18.

Step 1: Start from original data.

Customer	Age	Income	Gender	…	Response
Emma	28	1,000	F		No
Will	44	1,500	M		Yes
Dan	30	1,200	M		No
Bob	58	2,400	M		Yes

Step 2: Build a neural network.

Step 3: Get the network predictions and add them to the data set.

Customer	Age	Income	Gender	Network Prediction	Response
Emma	28	1,000	F	No	No
Will	44	1,500	M	Yes	Yes
Dan	30	1,200	M	Yes	No
Bob	58	2,400	M	Yes	Yes

Step 4: Extract rules relating network predictions to original inputs. Generate additional data where necessary.

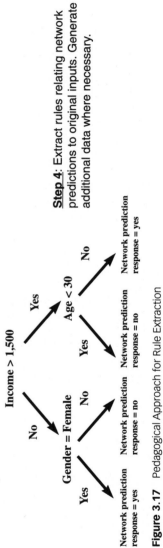

Figure 3.17 Pedagogical Approach for Rule Extraction

Step 1: Start from original data.

Customer	Age	Income	Gender	...	Response
Emma	28	1,000	F		No
Will	44	1,500	M		Yes
Dan	30	1,200	M		No
Bob	58	2,400	M		Yes

Step 2: Build logistic regression model.

Customer	Age	Income	Gender	...	Response	Logistic Regression Output
Emma	28	1,000	F		No (=0)	0.44
Will	44	1,500	M		Yes (=1)	0.76
Dan	30	1,200	M		No (=0)	0.18
Bob	58	2,400	M		Yes (=1)	0.88

Step 3: Calculate errors from logistic regression model.

Customer	Age	Income	Gender	...	Response	Logistic Regression Output	Error
Emma	28	1,000	F		No (=0)	0.44	-0.44
Will	44	1,500	M		Yes (=1)	0.76	0.24
Dan	30	1,200	M		No (=0)	0.18	-0.18
Bob	58	2,400	M		Yes (=1)	0.88	0.12

Step 4: Build NN predicting errors from logistic regression model.

Step 5: Score new observations by adding up logistic regression and NN scores.

Customer	Age	Income	Gender	...	Logistic Regression Output	NN Output	Final Output
Bart	28	1,000	F		0.68	-0.32	0.36

Figure 3.18 Two-Stage Models

SUPPORT VECTOR MACHINES

Two key shortcomings of neural networks are the fact that the objective function is nonconvex (and hence may have multiple local minima) and the effort that is needed to tune the number of hidden neurons. Support vector machines (SVMs) deal with both of these issues.[21]

The origins of classification SVMs date back to the early dates of linear programming.[22] Consider the following linear program (LP) for classification:

$$\min e_1 + e_2 + \cdots + e_{n_g} + \cdots + e_{n_b}$$

subject to

$$w_1 x_{i1} + w_2 x_{i2} + \cdots + w_n x_{in} \geq c - e_i, 1 \leq i \leq n_g$$

$$w_1 x_{i1} + w_2 x_{i2} + \cdots + w_n x_{in} \leq c + e_i, n_g + 1 \leq i \leq n_g + n_b$$

$$e_i \geq 0$$

The LP assigns the good customers a score above the cut-off value c, and the bad customers a score below c. n_g and n_b represent the number of goods and bads, respectively. The error variables e_i are needed to be able to solve the program because perfect separation will typically not be possible. Linear programming has been very popular in the early days of credit scoring. One of its benefits is that it is easy to include domain or business knowledge by adding extra constraints to the model.

A key problem with linear programming is that it can estimate multiple optimal decision boundaries, as illustrated in Figure 3.19, for a perfectly linearly separable case.

SVMs add an extra objective to the analysis. Consider, for example, the situation depicted in Figure 3.20. It has two hyperplanes sitting at the edges of both classes and a hyperplane in between, which will serve as the classification boundary. The perpendicular distance from the first hyperplane H1 to the origin equals $|b-1|/\|w\|$, whereby $\|w\|$ represents the Euclidean norm of w calculated as $\|w\| = \sqrt{w_1^2 + w_2^2}$. Likewise, the perpendicular distance from H2 to the origin equals $|b + 1|/\|w\|$. Hence, the margin between both hyperplanes equals $2/\|w\|$. SVMs will now aim at maximizing this margin to pull both classes as far apart as possible. Maximizing the margin is similar to minimizing

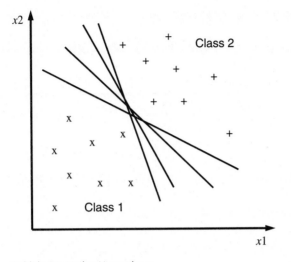

Figure 3.19 Multiple Separating Hyperplanes

$\|w\|$, or minimizing $\dfrac{1}{2}\displaystyle\sum_{i=1}^{N} w_i^2$. In case of perfect linear separation, the SVM classifier then becomes as follows.

Consider a training set: $\{x_k, y_k\}_{k=1}^{n}$ with $x_k \in R^N$ and $y_k \in \{-1; +1\}$

The goods (e.g., class +1) should be above hyperplane H1, and the bads (e.g., class−1) below hyperplane H2, which gives:

$$w^T x_k + b \geq 1, \; if \; y_k = +1$$

$$w^T x_k + b \leq 1, \; if \; y_k = -1$$

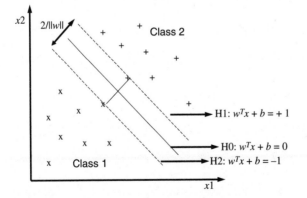

Figure 3.20 SVM Classifier for the Perfectly Linearly Separable Case

Both can be combined as follows:

$$y_k(w^T x_k + b) \geq 1$$

The optimization problem then becomes:

$$Minimize \frac{1}{2} \sum_{i=1}^{N} w_i^2$$

subject to $y_k(w^T x_k + b) \geq 1, k = 1...n$

This quadratic programming (QP) problem can now be solved using Lagrangian optimization.[23] It is important to note that the optimization problem has a quadratic cost function, giving a convex optimization problem with no local minima and only one global minimum. Training points that lie on one of the hyperplanes H1 or H2 are called *support vectors* and are essential to the classification. The classification hyperplane itself is H0 and, for new observations, it needs to be checked whether they are situated above H0, in which case the prediction is +1 or below (prediction −1). This can be easily accomplished using the sign operator as follows: $y(x) = sign (w^T x + b)$.

The SVM classifier discussed thus far assumed perfect separation is possible, which will of course rarely be the case for real-life data sets. In case of overlapping class distributions (as illustrated in Figure 3.21), the SVM classifier can be extended with error terms as follows:

$$Minimize \frac{1}{2} \sum_{i=1}^{N} w_i^2 + C \sum_{i=1}^{n} e_i$$

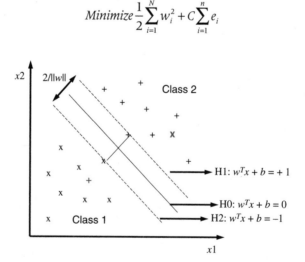

Figure 3.21   SVM Classifier in Case of Overlapping Distributions

subject to $y_k(w^T x_k + b) \geq 1 - e_k, k = 1 \dots n$

$$e_k \geq 0.$$

The error variables e_k are needed to allow for misclassifications. The C hyperparameter in the objective function balances the importance of maximizing the margin versus minimizing the error on the data. A high (low) value of C implies a higher (lower) risk of overfitting. We will come back to it in due course. Note that again a quadratic programming (QP) problem is obtained that can be solved using Lagrangian optimization.

Finally, the nonlinear SVM classifier will first map the input data to a higher dimensional feature space using some mapping $\varphi(x)$. This is illustrated in Figure 3.22.

The SVM problem formulation now becomes:

$$Minimize \frac{1}{2} \sum_{i=1}^{N} w_i^2 + C \sum_{i=1}^{n} e_i$$

subject to $y_k(w^T \varphi(x_k) + b) \geq 1 - e_k, k = 1 \dots n$

$$e_k \geq 0.$$

When working out the Lagrangian optimization,[24] it turns out that the mapping $\varphi(x)$ is never explicitly needed, but only implicitly by means of the kernel function K defined as follows: $K(x_k, x_l) = \varphi(x_k)^T \varphi(x_l)$.

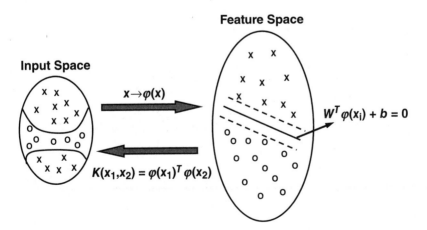

Figure 3.22 The Feature Space Mapping

Hence, the feature space does not need to be explicitly specified. The nonlinear SVM classifier then becomes:

$$y(x) = sign\left[\sum_{k=1}^{n}\alpha_k y_k K(x,x_k)+b\right]$$

whereby α_k are the Lagrangian multipliers stemming from the optimization. Support vectors will have nonzero α_k since they are needed to construct the classification line. All other observations have zero α_k, which is often referred to as the *sparseness property* of SVMs. Different types of kernel functions can be used. The most popular are:

- Linear kernel: $K(x,x_k) = x_k^T x$

- Polynomial kernel: $K(x,x_k) = (1+x_k^T x)^d$

- Radial basis function (RBF) kernel: $K(x,x_k) = \exp\{-\|x-x_k\|^2/\sigma^2\}$

Empirical evidence has shown that the RBF kernel usually performs best, but note that it includes an extra parameter σ to be tuned.[25]

An SVM classifier can be very easily represented as a neural network, as depicted in Figure 3.23.

The hidden layer uses, for example, RBF activation functions, whereas the output layer uses a linear activation function. Note that the number of hidden neurons now corresponds to the number of support vectors and follows automatically from the optimization. This is in strong contrast to neural networks where the number of hidden neurons needs to be tuned manually.

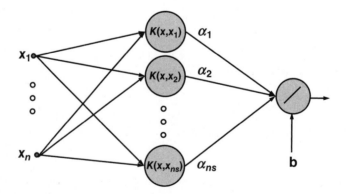

Figure 3.23   Representing an SVM Classifier as a Neural Network

A key question to answer when building SVM classifiers is the tuning of the hyperparameters. For example, suppose one has an RBF SVM that has two hyperparameters, C and σ. Both can be tuned using the following procedure:[26]

■ Partition the data into 40/30/30 percent training, validation, and test data.

■ Build an RBF SVM classifier for each (σ, C) combination from the sets $\sigma \in \{0.5, 5, 10, 15, 25, 50, 100, 250, 500\}$ and $C \in \{0.01, 0.05, 0.1, 0.5, 1, 5, 10, 50, 100, 500\}$.

■ Choose the (σ, C) combination with the best validation set performance.

■ Build an RBF SVM classifier with the optimal (σ, C) combination on the combined training + validation data set.

■ Calculate the performance of the estimated RBF SVM classifier on the test set.

In case of linear or polynomial kernels, a similar procedure can be adopted.

SVMs can also be used for regression applications with a continuous target. The idea here is to find a function $f(x)$ that has at most ε deviation from the actual targets y_i for all the training data, and is at the same time as flat as possible. Hence, errors less (higher) than ε will be tolerated (penalized). This is visualized in Figure 3.24.

Consider a training set: $\{x_k, y_k\}_{k=1}^n$ with $x_k \in R^N$ and $y_k \in R$

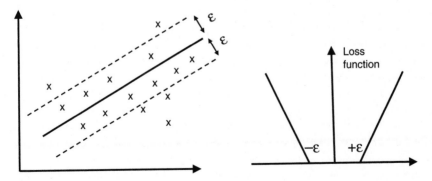

Figure 3.24 SVMs for Regression

The SVM formulation then becomes:

$$Minimize \frac{1}{2}\sum_{i=1}^{N} w_i^2 + C\sum_{i=1}^{n}(\varepsilon_k + \varepsilon_k^*)$$

subject to

$$y_k - w^T\varphi(x_k) - b \leq \varepsilon + \varepsilon_k$$

$$w^T\varphi(x_k) + b - y_k \leq \varepsilon + \varepsilon_k^*$$

$$\varepsilon, \varepsilon_k, \varepsilon_k^* \geq 0.$$

The hyperparameter C determines the trade-off between the flatness of f and the amount to which deviations larger than ε are tolerated. Note the feature space mapping $\varphi(x)$, which is also used here. Using Lagrangian optimization, the resulting nonlinear regression function becomes:

$$f(x) = \sum_{i=1}^{n}(\alpha_k - \alpha_k^*)K(x_k, x) + b,$$

whereby α_k and α_k^* represent the Lagrangian multipliers. The hyperparameters C and ε can be tuned using a procedure similar to the one outlined for classification SVMs.

Just as with neural networks, SVMs have a universal approximation property. As an extra benefit, they do not require tuning of the number of hidden neurons and are characterized by convex optimization. However, they are also very complex to be used in settings where interpretability is important. Since an SVM can be represented as a neural network (see Figure 3.23), one could use any of the rule extraction methods (decompositional, pedagogical) discussed in the section on neural networks to make them more comprehensible.[27] Also, two-stage models could be used to achieve this aim, whereby a second-stage SVM is estimated to correct for the errors of a simple (e.g., linear or logistic regression) model.

ENSEMBLE METHODS

Ensemble methods aim at estimating multiple analytical models instead of using only one. The idea here is that multiple models can cover different parts of the data input space and, as such, complement each other's deficiencies. In order to successfully accomplish this, the analytical technique needs to be sensitive to changes in the underlying data. This is especially the case for decision trees, and that's why they are commonly used in ensemble methods. In what follows, we will discuss bagging, boosting, and random forests.

Bagging

Bagging (bootstrap aggregating) starts by taking B bootstraps from the underlying sample.[28] Note that a bootstrap is a sample with replacement (see section on evaluating predictive models). The idea is then to build a classifier (e.g., decision tree) for every bootstrap. For classification, a new observation will be classified by letting all B classifiers vote, using, for example, a majority voting scheme whereby ties are resolved arbitrarily. For regression, the prediction is the average of the outcome of the B models (e.g., regression trees). Also note that here a standard error, and thus confidence interval, can be calculated. The number of bootstraps B can either be fixed (e.g., 30) or tuned via an independent validation data set.

The key element for bagging to be successful is the instability of the analytical techniques. If perturbing the data set by means of the bootstrapping procedure can alter the model constructed, then bagging will improve the accuracy.[29]

Boosting

Boosting works by estimating multiple models using a weighted sample of the data.[30] Starting from uniform weights, boosting will iteratively reweight the data according to the classification error, whereby misclassified cases get higher weights. The idea here is that difficult observations should get more attention. Either the analytical technique can directly work with weighted observations or, if not, we can just sample a new data set according to the weight distribution. The final ensemble model is then a weighted combination of all the individual models. A popular implementation of this is the adaptive boosting/adaboost procedure, which works as follows:

1. Given the following observations: (x_1, y_1), ..., (x_n, y_n) where x_i is the attribute vector of observation i and $y_i \in \{1, -1\}$
2. Initialize the weights as follows: $W_1(i) = 1/n$, $i = 1, ..., n$

3. For $t = 1...T$

    a. Train a weak classifier (e.g., decision tree) using the weights W_t

    b. Get weak classifier C_t with classification error ε_t

    c. Choose $\alpha_t = \dfrac{1}{2}\ln\left(\dfrac{1-\varepsilon_t}{\varepsilon_t}\right)$

    d. Update the weights as follows:

        i. $W_{t+1}(i) = \dfrac{W_t(i)}{Z_t}e^{-\alpha_t}$ if $C_t(x) = y_i$

        ii. $W_{t+1}(i) = \dfrac{W_t(i)}{Z_t}e^{\alpha_t}$ if $C_t(x) \neq y_i$

4. Output the final ensemble model: $E(x) = sign\left(\displaystyle\sum_{t=1}^{T}(\alpha_t C_t(x))\right)$

Note that in the above procedure, T represents the number of boosting runs, α_t measures the importance that is assigned to classifier C_t and increases as ε_t gets smaller, Z_t is a normalization factor needed to make sure that the weights in step t make up a distribution and as such sum to 1, and $C_t(x)$ represents the classification of the classifier built in step t for observation x. Multiple loss functions may be used to calculate the error ε_t, although the misclassification rate is undoubtedly the most popular. In substep i of step d, it can be seen that correctly classified observations get lower weights, whereas substep ii assigns higher weights to the incorrectly classified cases. Again, the number of boosting runs T can be fixed or tuned using an independent validation set. Note that various variants of this adaboost procedure exist, such as adaboost.M1, adaboost.M2 (both for multiclass classification), and adaboost.R1 and adaboost.R2 (both for regression).[31] A key advantage of boosting is that it is really easy to implement. A potential drawback is that there may be a risk of overfitting to the hard (potentially noisy) examples in the data, which will get higher weights as the algorithm proceeds.

Random Forests

Random forests was first introduced by Breiman.[32] It creates a forest of decision trees as follows:

1. Given a data set with n observations and N inputs
2. m = constant chosen on beforehand

3. For $t = 1,\ldots, T$

    a. Take a bootstrap sample with n observations

    b. Build a decision tree whereby for each node of the tree, randomly choose m inputs on which to base the splitting decision

    c. Split on the best of this subset

    d. Fully grow each tree without pruning

Common choices for m are 1, 2, or $floor(\log_2(N) + 1)$, which is recommended. Random forests can be used with both classification trees and regression trees. Key in this approach is the dissimilarity amongst the base classifiers (i.e., decision trees), which is obtained by adopting a bootstrapping procedure to select the training samples of the individual base classifiers, the selection of a random subset of attributes at each node, and the strength of the individual base models. As such, the diversity of the base classifiers creates an ensemble that is superior in performance compared to the single models.

More recently, an alternative to random forests was proposed: rotation forests. This ensemble technique takes the idea of random forests one step further. It combines the idea of pooling a large number of decision trees built on a subset of the attributes and data, with the application of principal component analysis prior to decision tree building, explaining its name. Rotating the axes prior to model building was found to enhance base classifier accuracy at the expense of losing the ability of ranking individual attributes by their importance.[33]

Empirical evidence has shown that random forests can achieve excellent predictive performance at the cost of decreased comprehensibility.

MULTICLASS CLASSIFICATION TECHNIQUES

All of the techniques previously discussed can be easily extended to a multiclass setting, whereby more than two target classes are available.

Multiclass Logistic Regression

When estimating a multiclass logistic regression model, one first needs to know whether the target variable is nominal or ordinal. Examples of nominal targets could be predicting blood type and predicting voting behavior. Examples of ordinal targets could be predicting credit ratings and predicting income as high, medium, or low.

For nominal target variables, one of the target classes (say class K) will be chosen as the base class as follows:

$$\frac{P(Y = 1 | X_1, \ldots, X_N)}{P(Y = K | X_1, \ldots, X_N)} = e^{\left(\beta_0^1 + \beta_1^1 X_1 + \beta_2^1 X_2 + \cdots \beta_N^1 X_N\right)}$$

$$\frac{P(Y = 2 | X_1, \ldots, X_N)}{P(Y = K | X_1, \ldots, X_N)} = e^{\left(\beta_0^2 + \beta_1^2 X_1 + \beta_2^2 X_2 + \cdots \beta_N^2 X_N\right)}$$

$$\cdots$$

$$\frac{P(Y = K - 1 | X_1, \ldots, X_N)}{P(Y = K | X_1, \ldots, X_N)} = e^{\left(\beta_0^{K-1} + \beta_1^{K-1} X_1 + \beta_2^{K-1} X_2 + \cdots \beta_N^{K-1} X_N\right)}$$

Using the fact that all probabilities must sum to 1, one can obtain the following:

$$P(Y = 1 | X_1, \ldots, X_N) = \frac{e^{\left(\beta_0^1 + \beta_1^1 X_1 + \beta_2^1 X_2 + \cdots \beta_N^1 X_N\right)}}{1 + \sum_{k=1}^{K-1} e^{\left(\beta_0^k + \beta_1^k X_1 + \beta_2^k X_2 + \cdots \beta_N^k X_N\right)}}$$

$$P(Y = 2 | X_1, \ldots, X_N) = \frac{e^{\left(\beta_0^2 + \beta_1^2 X_1 + \beta_2^2 X_2 + \cdots \beta_N^2 X_N\right)}}{1 + \sum_{k=1}^{K-1} e^{\left(\beta_0^k + \beta_1^k X_1 + \beta_2^k X_2 + \cdots \beta_N^k X_N\right)}}$$

$$P(Y = K | X_1, \ldots, X_N) = \frac{1}{1 + \sum_{k=1}^{K-1} e^{\left(\beta_0^k + \beta_1^k X_1 + \beta_2^k X_2 + \cdots \beta_N^k X_N\right)}}$$

The β parameters are then usually estimated using maximum aposteriori estimation, which is an extension of maximum likelihood estimation. As with binary logistic regression, the procedure comes with standard errors, confidence intervals, and p-values.

In case of ordinal targets, one could estimate a cumulative logistic regression as follows:

$$P(Y \leq 1) = \frac{1}{1 + e^{-\theta_1 + \beta_1 X_1 + \cdots + \beta_N X_N}}$$

$$P(Y \leq 2) = \frac{1}{1 + e^{-\theta_2 + \beta_1 X_1 + \cdots + \beta_N X_N}}$$

$$\cdots$$

$$P(Y \leq K - 1) = \frac{1}{1 + e^{-\theta_{K-1} + \beta_1 X_1 + \cdots + \beta_N X_N}}$$

or,

$$\frac{P(Y \leq 1)}{1 - P(Y \leq 1)} = e^{-\theta_1 + \beta_1 X_1 + \cdots + \beta_N X_N}$$

$$\frac{P(Y \leq 2)}{1 - P(Y \leq 2)} = e^{-\theta_2 + \beta_1 X_1 + \cdots + \beta_N X_N}$$

$$\cdots$$

$$\frac{P(Y \leq K - 1)}{1 - P(Y \leq K - 1)} = e^{-\theta_{K-1} + \beta_1 X_1 + \cdots + \beta_N X_N}$$

Note that since $P(Y \leq K) = 1$, $\theta_K = +\infty$.

The individual probabilities can then be obtained as follows:

$$P(Y = 1) = P(Y \leq 1)$$

$$P(Y = 2) = P(Y \leq 2) - P(Y \leq 1)$$

$$\cdots$$

$$P(Y = K) = 1 - P(Y \leq K - 1)$$

Also for this model, the β parameters can be estimated using a maximum likelihood procedure.

Multiclass Decision Trees

Decision trees can be easily extended to a multiclass setting. For the splitting decision, assuming K classes, the impurity criteria become:

$$Entropy(S) = -\sum_{k=1}^{K} p_k log_2(p_k)$$

$$Gini(S) = \sum_{k=1}^{K} p_k(1 - p_k)$$

The stopping decision can be made in a similar way as for binary target decision trees by using an independent validation data set. The assignment decision then looks for the most prevalent class in each of the leaf nodes.

Multiclass Neural Networks

A straightforward option for training a multiclass neural network for K classes, is to create K output neurons, one for each class. An observation is then assigned to the output neuron with the highest activation value (winner take all learning). Another option is to use a softmax activation function.[34]

Multiclass Support Vector Machines

A common practice to estimate a multiclass support vector machine is to map the multiclass classification problem to a set of binary classification problems. Two well-known schemes here are one-versus-one and one-versus-all coding.[35]

For K classes, one-versus-one coding estimates $K(K - 1)/2$ binary SVM classifiers contrasting every possible pair of classes. Every classifier as such can cast a vote on the target class and the final classification is then the result of a (weighted) voting procedure. Ties are resolved arbitrarily. This is illustrated in Figure 3.25.

For K classes, one-versus-all coding estimates K binary SVM classifiers each time contrasting one particular class against all the other ones. A classification decision can then be made by assigning a particular observation to the class for which one of the binary classifiers assigns the highest posterior probability. Ties are less likely to occur with this scheme. This is illustrated in Figure 3.26.

Note that one-versus-one and one-versus-all are meta schemes that can be used with other base classifiers as well.

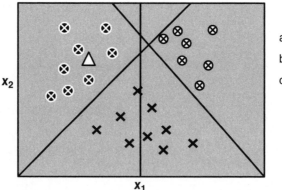

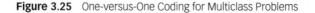

Figure 3.25   One-versus-One Coding for Multiclass Problems

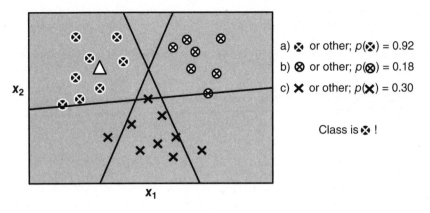

a) ⊗ or other; $p(⊗) = 0.92$
b) ⊗ or other; $p(⊗) = 0.18$
c) ✗ or other; $p(✗) = 0.30$

Class is ⊗ !

Figure 3.26 One-versus-All Coding for Multiclass Problems

EVALUATING PREDICTIVE MODELS

In this section, we will discuss how to evaluate the performance of predictive models. First, we will discuss how to split up the data set. This will be followed by a discussion of performance metrics.

Splitting Up the Data Set

When evaluating predictive models, two key decisions need to be made. A first decision concerns the data set split up, which specifies on what part of the data the performance will be measured. A second decision concerns the performance metric. In what follows, we will elaborate on both.

The decision how to split up the data set for performance measurement depends upon its size. In case of large data sets (say more than 1,000 observations), the data can be split up into a training and a test sample. The training sample (also called *development* or *estimation sample*) will be used to build the model, whereas the test sample (also called the *hold out sample*) will be used to calculate its performance (see Figure 3.27). There should be a strict separation between training and test sample. Note that in case of decision trees or neural networks, the validation sample should be part of the training sample because it is actively being used during model development (i.e., to make the stopping decision).

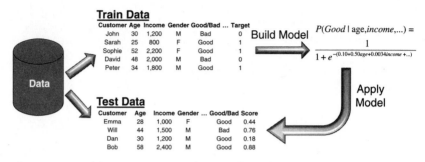

Figure 3.27   Training versus Test Sample Set Up for Performance Estimation

In the case of small data sets (say, less than 1,000 observations), special schemes need to be adopted. A very popular scheme is cross-validation (see Figure 3.28). In cross-validation, the data is split into K folds (e.g., 10). A model is then trained on $K - 1$ training folds and tested on the remaining validation fold. This is repeated for all possible validation folds resulting in K performance estimates that can then be averaged. Note also that a standard deviation and/or confidence interval can be calculated if desired. Common choices for K are 5 and 10. In its most extreme case, cross-validation becomes leave-one-out cross-validation whereby every observation is left out in turn and a model is estimated on the remaining $K - 1$ observations. This gives K analytical models in total. In stratified cross-validation, special care is taken to make sure the good/bad odds are the same in each fold.

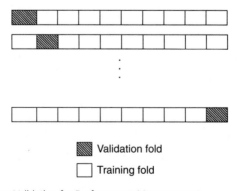

Figure 3.28   Cross-Validation for Performance Measurement

A key question to answer when doing cross-validation is what should be the final model that is being output from the procedure. Because cross-validation gives multiple models, this is not an obvious question. Of course, one could let all models collaborate in an ensemble setup. A more pragmatic answer would be to, for example, do leave-one-out cross-validation and pick one of the models at random. Because the models differ up to one observation, they will be quite similar anyway. Alternatively, one may also choose to build one final model on all observations but report the performance coming out of the cross-validation procedure as the best independent estimate.

For small samples, one may also adopt bootstrapping procedures. In bootstrapping, one takes samples with replacement from a data set D (see Figure 3.29).

The probability that a customer is not sampled equals $1/n$, with n being the number of observations in the data set. Assuming a bootstrap with n samples, the fraction of customers that is not sampled equals:

$$\left(1-\frac{1}{n}\right)^n.$$

We then have:

$$\lim_{n\to\infty}\left(1-\frac{1}{n}\right)^n = e^{-1} = 0.368$$

whereby the approximation already works well for small values of n. So, 0.368 is the probability that a customer does not appear in the sample and 0.632 is the probability that a customer does appear. If we then take the bootstrap sample as the training set, and the test set as all samples in D but not in the bootstrap, we can calculate the performance as follows:

Error estimate = 0.368 error(training) + 0.632 error(test),

whereby obviously a higher weight is being put on the test set performance.

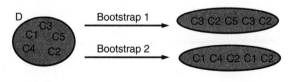

Figure 3.29 Bootstrapping

Table 3.3 Example Data Set for Performance Calculation

	Churn	Score
John	Yes	0.72
Sophie	No	0.56
David	Yes	0.44
Emma	No	0.18
Bob	No	0.36

Performance Measures for Classification Models

Consider, for example, the following churn prediction example for a five customer data set. The first column in Table 3.3 depicts the true status, whereas the second column is the churn score as it comes from a logistic regression, decision tree, neural network, and so on.

One can now map the scores to a predicted classification label by assuming a default cutoff of 0.5 as shown in Figure 3.30.

A confusion matrix can now be calculated and is shown in Table 3.4.

Based upon this matrix, one can now calculate the following performance measures:

- Classification accuracy = $(TP + TN)/(TP + FP + FN + TN) = 3/5$
- Classification error = $(FP + FN)/(TP + FP + FN + TN) = 2/5$
- Sensitivity = $TP/(TP + FN) = 1/2$
- Specificity = $TN/(FP + TN) = 2/3$

However, note that all these classification measures depend on the cut-off. For example, for a cut off of 0 (1), classification accuracy

	Churn	Score			Churn	Score	Predicted
John	Yes	0.72		John	Yes	0.72	Yes
Sophie	No	0.56	Cutoff = 0.50	Sophie	No	0.56	Yes
David	Yes	0.44	⟶	David	Yes	0.44	No
Emma	No	0.18		Emma	No	0.18	No
Bob	No	0.36		Bob	No	0.36	No

Figure 3.30 Calculating Predictions Using a Cut-Off

Table 3.4 The Confusion Matrix

		Actual Status	
		Positive (churn)	Negative (no churn)
Predicted status	Positive (churn)	True positive (John)	False positive (Sophie)
	Negative (no churn)	False negative (David)	True negative (Emma, Bob)

becomes 40 percent (60 percent), the error 60 percent (40 percent), the sensitivity 100 percent (0), and the specificity 0 (100 percent). It would be nice to have a performance measure that is independent from the cut-off. One could construct a table with the sensitivity, specificity, and 1−specificity for various cut-offs as shown in Table 3.5.

The receiver operating characteristic (ROC) curve then plots the sensitivity versus 1−specificity as illustrated in Figure 3.31.[36]

Note that a perfect model has a sensitivity of 1 and a specificity of 1, and is thus represented by the upper left corner. The closer the curve approaches this point, the better the performance. In Figure 3.31, scorecard A has a better performance than scorecard B. A problem arises, however, if the curves intersect. In this case, one can calculate the area under the ROC curve (AUC) as a performance metric. The AUC provides a simple figure-of-merit for the performance of the constructed classifier. The higher the AUC, the better the performance. The AUC is always bounded between 0 and 1 and can be interpreted as a probability. In fact, it represents the probability that a randomly chosen churner gets a higher score than a randomly chosen nonchurner.[37] Note that the diagonal represents a random scorecard whereby sensitivity equals 1−specificity for all cut off points. Hence, a

Table 3.5 ROC Analysis

Cutoff	Sensitivity	Specificity	1−Specificity
0	1	0	1
0.01			
0.02			
....			
0.99			
1	0	1	0

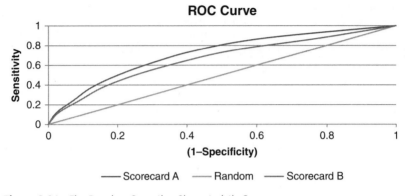

Figure 3.31 The Receiver Operating Characteristic Curve

good classifier should have an ROC above the diagonal and AUC bigger than 50%. Table 3.6 presents some AUC benchmarks for various analytics applications.[38]

A lift curve is another important performance metric. It starts by sorting the population from low score to high score. Suppose now that in the top 10% lowest scores there are 60 percent bads, whereas the total population has 10% bads. The lift value in the top decile then becomes 60/10 percent or 6. In other words, the lift value represents the cumulative percentage of bads per decile, divided by the overall population percentage of bads. Using no model, or a random sorting, the bads would be equally spread across the entire range and the lift value would always equal 1. Obviously, the lift curve always decreases as one considers bigger deciles, until it will reach 1. This is illustrated in Figure 3.32. Note that a lift curve can also be expressed in a noncumulative way, and is also often summarized as the top decile lift.

Table 3.6 Performance Benchmarks in Terms of AUC

Application	Number of Characteristics	AUC Ranges
Application credit scoring	10–15	70–85%
Behavioral credit scoring	10–15	80–90%
Churn detection (telco)	6–10	70–90%
Fraud detection (insurance)	10–15	70–90%

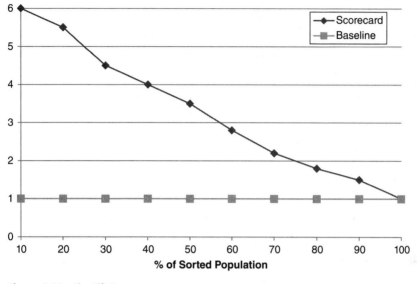

Figure 3.32 The Lift Curve

The cumulative accuracy profile (CAP), Lorenz, or power curve is very closely related to the lift curve (see Figure 3.33). It also starts by sorting the population from low score to high score and then measures the cumulative percentage of bads for each decile on the Y-axis. The perfect model gives a linearly increasing curve up to the sample bad rate and then flattens out. The diagonal again represents the random model.

The CAP curve can be summarized in an Accuracy Ratio (AR) as depicted in Figure 3.34.

The accuracy ratio is then defined as follows:

(Area below power curve for current model–Area below power curve for random model)/

(Area below power curve for perfect model–Area below power curve for random model)

A perfect model will thus have an AR of 1 and a random model an AR of 0. Note that the accuracy ratio is also often referred to as the *Gini coefficient*. There is also a linear relation between the AR and the AUC as follows: $AR = 2 * AUC - 1$.

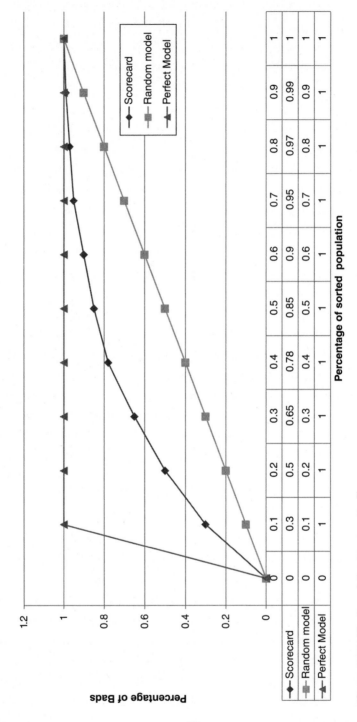

The following data accompanies the figure:

	0	0.1	0.2	0.3	0.4	0.5	0.6	0.7	0.8	0.9	1
Scorecard	0	0.3	0.5	0.65	0.78	0.85	0.9	0.95	0.97	0.99	1
Random model	0	0.1	0.2	0.3	0.4	0.5	0.6	0.7	0.8	0.9	1
Perfect Model	0	1	1	1	1	1	1	1	1	1	1

Figure 3.33 The Cumulative Accuracy Profile

78

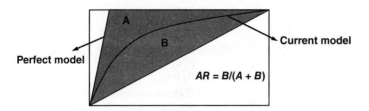

Figure 3.34 Calculating the Accuracy Ratio

The Kolmogorov-Smirnov distance is a separation measure calculating the maximum distance between the cumulative score distributions P(s|B) and P(s|G) defined as follows (see Figure 3.35):

$$P(s|G) = \sum_{x \leq s} p(x|G)$$

$$P(s|B) = \sum_{x \leq s} p(x|B)$$

Note that by definition $P(s|G)$ equals 1–sensitivity, and $P(s|B)$ equals the specificity. Hence, it can easily be verified that the KS distance can also be measured on an ROC graph. It fact, it is equal to the maximum vertical distance between the ROC curve and the diagonal.

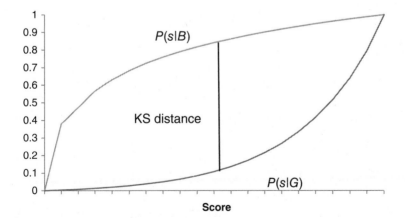

Figure 3.35 The Kolmogorov-Smirnov Statistic

Another performance measure is the Mahalanobis distance between the score distributions, defined as follows:

$$M = \frac{|\mu_G - \mu_B|}{\sigma},$$

whereby μ_G (μ_B) represents the mean score of the goods (bads) and σ the pooled standard deviation. Obviously, a high Mahalanobis distance is preferred because it means both score distributions are well separated. Closely related is the divergence metric, calculated as follows:

$$D = \frac{(\mu_G - \mu_B)^2}{\frac{1}{2}(\sigma_G^2 + \sigma_B^2)}$$

In case of multiclass targets, other performance measures need to be adopted. Figure 3.36 presents an example of a multiclass confusion matrix.

The on-diagonal elements represented in gray correspond to the correct classifications. Off-diagonal elements represent errors. Note, however, that not all errors have equal impact. Given the ordinal nature of the target variable, the further away from the diagonal, the bigger the impact of the error. For example, in Figure 3.36, there are 34 C+ observations predicted as C, which is not as bad as the one C+ predicted as D. One could summarize this in a notch difference graph that depicts the cumulative accuracy for increasing notch differences. Figure 3.37 gives an example of a notch difference graph.

At the 0 notch difference level, the performance equals about 35 percent, which may not seem very good. However, by allowing for a one-notch difference, the performance almost doubles to around 75 percent, which is a lot better!

The AUC can be generalized to the multiclass setting by plotting an ROC graph for each class against all other classes, calculating the AUC, and taking the overall average. Another option is to calculate an AUC for each possible class comparison and then take the average.[39]

	Predicted														
True	A+	A	A-	B+	B	B-	C+	C	C-	D+	D	D-	E+	E	E-
A+	0	0	0	0	0	0	0	0	0	0	0	0	0	0	0
A	0	14	0	4	0	0	0	0	0	0	0	0	0	0	0
A-	0	0	0	2	0	0	0	0	0	0	0	0	0	0	0
B+	0	7	0	50	0	0	5	5	0	1	0	0	1	0	0
B	0	2	2	54	0	12	58	17	0	5	1	0	0	0	0
B-	0	0	0	6	0	6	10	6	0	1	1	0	0	0	0
C+	0	1	0	13	0	3	99	34	0	11	4	0	0	0	0
C	0	0	0	5	0	1	37	151	1	12	0	0	0	0	0
C-	0	0	0	2	0	0	3	8	3	4	0	0	3	1	0
D+	0	0	0	1	0	0	7	20	2	131	24	0	13	7	0
D	0	0	0	0	0	0	2	9	1	32	122	2	1	0	0
D-	0	0	0	0	0	0	0	0	0	0	0	0	0	0	0
E+	0	0	0	0	0	0	0	4	0	12	26	0	37	5	0
E	0	0	0	0	0	0	0	4	0	4	9	0	5	48	0
E-	0	0	0	0	0	0	0	0	0	0	0	0	0	0	0

Figure 3.36 Confusion Matrix for a Multiclass Example

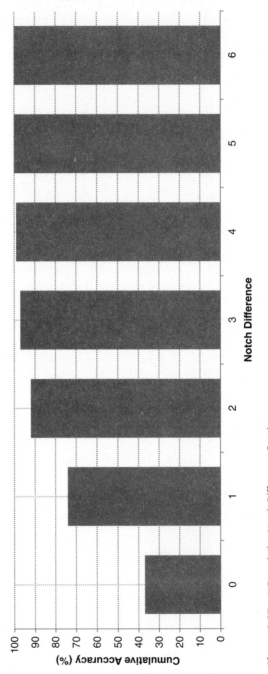

Figure 3.37 A Cumulative Notch Difference Graph

Performance Measures for Regression Models

Multiple measures exist to calculate the performance of regression models. A first key metric is the R-squared, defined as follows:

$$R^2 = 1 - \frac{\sum_{i=1}^{n}(y_i - \hat{y}_i)^2}{\sum_{i=1}^{n}(y_i - \bar{y})^2},$$

whereby y_i is the true value, $\hat{y}_i$ the predicted value, and $\bar{y}$ the average. The R^2 always varies between 0 and 1, and higher values are to be preferred. Two other popular measures are the mean squared error (MSE) and mean absolute deviation (MAD), defined as follows:

$$MSE = \frac{\sum_{i=1}^{n}(y_i - \hat{y}_i)^2}{n}$$

$$MAD = \frac{\sum_{i=1}^{n}|y_i - \hat{y}_i|}{n}$$

A scatter plot between the predicted and the target values can give a visual representation of model performance (see Figure 3.38). The more the plot approaches a straight line through the origin, the better the performance of the model. It can be summarized by calculating the Pearson correlation coefficient.

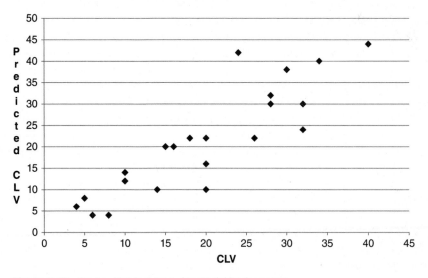

Figure 3.38 Scatter Plot for Measuring Model Performance

NOTES

1. T. Hastie, R. Tibshirani, and J. Friedman, *Elements of Statistical Learning: Data Mining, Inference and Prediction* (Springer-Verlag, Berlin, Germany, 2001).

2. S. Viaene et al., "A Comparison of State-of-the-Art Classification Techniques for Expert Automobile Insurance Fraud Detection." Special issue, *Journal of Risk and Insurance* 69, no. 3 (2002): 433–443.

3. S. Gupta et al., "Modeling Customer Lifetime Value," *Journal of Service Research* 9, no. 2 (2006): 139–155; N. Glady, C. Croux, and B. Baesens, "Modeling Churn Using Customer Lifetime Value," *European Journal of Operational Research* 197, no. 1 (2009): 402–411.

4. T. Van Gestel and B. Baesens, *Credit Risk Management: Basic Concepts: Financial Risk Components, Rating Analysis, Models, Economic and Regulatory Capital* (Oxford University Press, 2009); G. Loterman et al., "Benchmarking Regression Algorithms for Loss Given Default Modeling," *International Journal of Forecasting* 28, no. 1 (2012): 161–170; E. Tobback et al., "Forecasting Loss Given Default Models: Impact of Account Characteristics and the Macroeconomic State," *Journal of the Operational Research Society,* forthcoming 2014.

5. D. W. Dwyer, A. Kocagil, and R. Stein, *The Moody's KMV EDF™ RiskCalc™ v3.1 Model Next Generation Technology for Predicting Private Firm Credit Risk* (White paper, 2004).

6. R. O. Duda, P. E. Hart, and D. G. Stork, *Pattern Classification* (John Wiley & Sons, Hoboken, New Jersey, US, 2001).

7. J. R. Quinlan, *C4.5 Programs for Machine Learning* (Morgan Kauffman Publishers, Burlington, Massachusetts, United States, 1993).

8. L. Breiman et al., *Classification and Regression Trees* (Monterey, CA: Wadsworth & Brooks/Cole Advanced Books & Software, 1984).

9. J. A. Hartigan, *Clustering Algorithms* (New York: John Wiley & Sons, 1975).

10. C. M. Bishop, *Neural Networks for Pattern Recognition* (Oxford University Press, Oxford, England, 1995); J. M. Zurada, *Introduction to Artificial Neural Systems* (Boston: PWS Publishing, 1992).

11. B. Baesens et al., "Bayesian Neural Network Learning for Repeat Purchase Modelling in Direct Marketing," *European Journal of Operational Research* 138, no. 1 (2002): 191–211.

12. K. Hornik, M. Stinchcombe, and H. White, "Multilayer Feedforward Networks Are Universal Approximators," *Neural Networks* 2, no. 5 (1989): 359–366.

13. See C. M. Bishop, *Neural Networks for Pattern Recognition* (Oxford University Press, Oxford, England, 1995) for more details.

14. J. Moody and J. Utans. "Architecture Selection Strategies for Neural Networks: Application to Corporate Bond Rating Prediction," in *Neural Networks in the Capital Markets,* A. N. Refenes (editor) (New York: John Wiley & Sons, 1994).

15. P. L. Bartlett, "For Valid Generalization, the Size of the Weights Is More Important than the Size of the Network," in *Advances in Neural Information Processing Systems 9,* ed. M. C, Mozer, M. I. Jordan, and T. Petsche (Cambridge, MA: MIT Press, 1997), 134–140.

16. B. Baesens, D. et al., "White Box Nonlinear Prediction Models." Special issue, *IEEE Transactions on Neural Networks* 22, no. 12 (2011): 2406–2408.

17. B. Baesens, "Developing Intelligent Systems for Credit Scoring using Machine Learning Techniques" (PhD thesis, Katholieke Universiteit Leuven, 2003); B. Baesens et al.,

"Using Neural Network Rule Extraction and Decision Tables for Credit-Risk Evaluation," *Management Science* 49, no. 3 (2003): 312–329; R. Setiono, B. Baesens, and C. Mues, "A Note on Knowledge Discovery Using Neural Networks and Its Application to Credit Card Screening," *European Journal of Operational Research* 192, no. 1 (2009): 326–332.

18. H. Lu, R. Setiono, and H. Liu, "NeuroRule: A Connectionist Approach to Data Mining," in *Proceedings of 21st International Conference on Very Large Data Bases* (Zurich, Switzerland, Morgan Kaufmann, 1995), 478–489.

19. M. Craven and J. Shavlik, "Extracting Tree-Structured Representations of Trained Networks," in *Advances in Neural Information Processing Systems* (Cambridge, MA: MIT Press, 1996).

20. T. Van Gestel et al., "Linear and Nonlinear Credit Scoring by Combining Logistic Regression and Support Vector Machines," *Journal of Credit Risk* 1, no. 4 (2005); T. Van Gestel et al., "A Process Model to Develop an Internal Rating System: Sovereign Credit Ratings," *Decision Support Systems* 42, no. 2 (2006): 1131–1151.

21. N. Cristianini and J. S. Taylor, *An Introduction to Support Vector Machines and Other Kernel-based Learning Methods* (Cambridge University Press, 2000); B. Schölkopf and A. Smola, *Learning with Kernels* (Cambridge, MA: MIT Press, 2001); V. Vapnik, *The Nature of Statistical Learning Theory* (New York: Springer-Verlag, 1995).

22. O. L. Mangasarian, "Linear and Non-linear Separation of Patterns by Linear Programming," *Operations Research* 13, May–June (1965): 444–452.

23. N. Cristianini and J. S. Taylor, *An Introduction to Support Vector Machines and Other Kernel-based Learning Methods* (Cambridge University Press, 2000); B. Schölkopf and A. Smola, *Learning with Kernels* (Cambridge, MA: MIT Press, 2001); V. Vapnik, *The Nature of Statistical Learning Theory* (New York: Springer-Verlag, 1995).

24. N. Cristianini and J. S. Taylor, *An Introduction to Support Vector Machines and Other Kernel-based Learning Methods* (Cambridge University Press, 2000); B. Schölkopf and A. Smola, *Learning with Kernels* (Cambridge, MA: MIT Press, 2001); V. Vapnik, *The Nature of Statistical Learning Theory* (New York: Springer-Verlag, 1995).

25. T. Van Gestel et al., "Benchmarking Least Squares Support Vector Machine Classifiers," *Machine Learning* 54, no. 1 (2004): 5–32.

26. Ibid.

27. D. Martens et al., "Comprehensible Credit Scoring Models Using Rule Extraction From Support Vector Machines," *European Journal of Operational Research* 183 (2007): 1466–1476; D. Martens, B. Baesens, and T. Van Gestel, "Decompositional Rule Extraction from Support Vector Machines by Active Learning," *IEEE Transactions on Knowledge and Data Engineering* 21, no. 1, (2009): 178–191.

28. L. Breiman, "Bagging Predictors," *Machine Learning* 24, no. 2 (1996): 123–140.

29. Ibid.

30. Y. Freund and R. E. Schapire, "A Decision-Theoretic Generalization of On-Line Learning and an Application to Boosting," *Journal of Computer and System Sciences* 55, no. 1 (1997): 119–139; Y. Freund and R. E. Schapire, "A Short Introduction to Boosting," *Journal of Japanese Society for Artificial Intelligence* 14, no. 5 (1999): 771–780.

31. See Y. Freund and R. E. Schapire, "A Decision-Theoretic Generalization of On-Line Learning and an Application to Boosting," *Journal of Computer and System Sciences* 55, no. 1 (1997): 119–139, and Y. Freund and R. E. Schapire, "A Short Introduction to Boosting," *Journal of Japanese Society for Artificial Intelligence* 14, no. 5 (1999): 771–780, for more details.

32. L. Breiman, "Random Forests," *Machine Learning* 45, no. 1 (2001): 5–32.

33. J. J. Rodriguez, L. I. Kuncheva, and C. J. Alonso, "Rotation Forest: A New Classifier Ensemble Method," *IEEE Transactions on Pattern Analysis and Machine Intelligence* 28, no. 10 (2006): 1619–1630.

34. C. M. Bishop, *Neural Networks for Pattern Recognition* (Oxford University Press, Oxford, England, 1995).

35. T. Van Gestel, "From Linear to Kernel Based Methods for Classification, Modelling and Prediction" (PhD Thesis, Katholieke Universiteit Leuven, 2002).

36. T. Fawcett, "ROC Graphs: Notes and Practical Considerations for Researchers," *HP Labs Tech Report HPL-2003–4*, HP Laboratories, Palo Alto, US (2003).

37. E. R. Delong, D. M. Delong, and D. L. Clarke-Pearson, "Comparing the Areas Under Two or More Correlated Receiver Operating Characteristic Curves: A Nonparametric Approach," *Biometrics* 44 (1988): 837–845; J. A, Hanley and B. J. McNeil, "The Meaning and Use of Area under the ROC Curve," *Radiology* 143 (1982): 29–36.

38. B. Baesens et al., "Benchmarking State of the Art Classification Algorithms for Credit Scoring," *Journal of the Operational Research Society* 54, no. 6 (2003): 627–635; W. Verbeke et al., "New Insights into Churn Prediction in the Telecommunication Sector: A Profit Driven Data Mining Approach," *European Journal of Operational Research* 218, no. 1 (2012): 211–229.

39. D. Hand and R. J. Till, "A Simple Generalization of the Area under the ROC Curve to Multiple Class Classification Problems," *Machine Learning* 45, no. 2 (2001): 171–186.

CHAPTER **4**

Descriptive Analytics

I n descriptive analytics, the aim is to describe patterns of customer behavior. Contrary to predictive analytics, there is no real target variable (e.g., churn or fraud indicator) available. Hence, descriptive analytics is often referred to as *unsupervised learning* because there is no target variable to steer the learning process. The three most common types of descriptive analytics are summarized in Table 4.1.

ASSOCIATION RULES

In this section, we will address how to mine association rules from data. First, the basic setting will be discussed. This will be followed by a discussion of support and confidence, which are two key measures for association rule mining. Next, we will zoom into the association rule mining process. The lift measure will then be introduced. The section will be concluded by discussing post processing, extensions, and various applications of association rules.

Basic Setting

Association rules typically start from a database of transactions, D. Each transaction consists of a transaction identifier and a set of items (e.g.,

Table 4.1 Examples of Descriptive Analytics

Type of Descriptive Analytics	Explanation	Example
Association rules	Detect frequently occurring patterns between items	Detecting what products are frequently purchased together in a supermarket context
		Detecting what words frequently co-occur in a text document
		Detecting what elective courses are frequently chosen together in a university setting
Sequence rules	Detect sequences of events	Detecting sequences of purchase behavior in a supermarket context
		Detecting sequences of web page visits in a web mining context
		Detecting sequences of words in a text document
Clustering	Detect homogeneous segments of observations	Differentiate between brands in a marketing portfolio
		Segment customer population for targeted marketing

products, Web pages, courses) $\{i_1, i_2, ..., i_n\}$ selected from all possible items (I). Table 4.2 gives an example of a transactions database in a supermarket setting.

An association rule is then an implication of the form $X \Rightarrow Y$, whereby $X \subset I$, $Y \subset I$ and $X \cap Y = \varnothing$. X is referred to as the rule

Table 4.2 Example Transaction Data Set

Transaction Identifier	Items
1	Beer, milk, diapers, baby food
2	Coke, beer, diapers
3	Cigarettes, diapers, baby food
4	Chocolates, diapers, milk, apples
5	Tomatoes, water, apples, beer
6	Spaghetti, diapers, baby food, beer
7	Water, beer, baby food
8	Diapers, baby food, spaghetti
9	Baby food, beer, diapers, milk
10	Apples, wine, baby food

antecedent, whereas Y is referred to as the rule consequent. Examples of association rules are:

- If a customer has a car loan and car insurance, then the customer has a checking account in 80% of the cases.
- If a customer buys spaghetti, then the customer buys red wine in 70 percent of the cases.
- If a customer visits web page A, then the customer will visit web page B in 90% of the cases.

It is hereby important to note that association rules are stochastic in nature, which means they should not be interpreted as a universal truth and are characterized by statistical measures quantifying the strength of the association. Also, the rules measure correlational associations and should not be interpreted in a causal way.

Support and Confidence

Support and confidence are two key measures to quantify the strength of an association rule. The support of an item set is defined as the percentage of total transactions in the database that contains the item set. Hence, the rule $X \Rightarrow Y$ has support (s) if $100s\%$ of the transactions in D contain $X \cup Y$. It can be formally defined as follows:

$$support(X \cup Y) = \frac{number\ of\ transactions\ supporting\ (X \cup Y)}{total\ number\ of\ transactions}$$

When considering the transaction database in Table 4.2, the association rule baby food and diapers $\Rightarrow$ beer has support 3/10 or 30 percent.

A frequent item set is one for which the support is higher than a threshold (minsup) that is typically specified upfront by the business user or data analyst. A lower (higher) support will obviously generate more (less) frequent item sets. The confidence measures the strength of the association and is defined as the conditional probability of the rule consequent, given the rule antecedent. The rule $X \Rightarrow Y$ has confidence (c) if $100c\%$ of the transactions in D that contain X also contain Y. It can be formally defined as follows:

$$confidence(X \rightarrow Y) = P(Y|X) = \frac{support(X \cup Y)}{support(X)}$$

Again, the data analyst has to specify a minimum confidence (minconf) in order for an association rule to be considered interesting.

When considering Table 4.2, the association rule baby food and diapers ⇒ beer has confidence 3/5 or 60 percent.

Association Rule Mining

Mining association rules from data is essentially a two-step process as follows:

1. Identification of all item sets having support above minsup (i.e., "frequent" item sets)

2. Discovery of all derived association rules having confidence above minconf

As said before, both minsup and minconf need to be specified beforehand by the data analyst. The first step is typically performed using the Apriori algorithm.[1] The basic notion of *a priori* states that every subset of a frequent item set is frequent as well or, conversely, every superset of an infrequent item set is infrequent. This implies that candidate item sets with k items can be found by pairwise joining frequent item sets with $k - 1$ items and deleting those sets that have infrequent subsets. Thanks to this property, the number of candidate subsets to be evaluated can be decreased, which will substantially improve the performance of the algorithm because fewer databases passes will be required. The Apriori algorithm is illustrated in Figure 4.1.

Once the frequent item sets have been found, the association rules can be generated in a straightforward way, as follows:

- For each frequent item set k, generate all nonempty subsets of k
- For every nonempty subset s of k, output the rule $s \Rightarrow k - s$ if the confidence > minconf

Note that the confidence can be easily computed using the support values that were obtained during the frequent item set mining.

For the frequent item set {baby food, diapers, beer}, the following association rules can be derived:

diapers, beer ⇒ baby food [*conf* = 75%]

baby food, beer ⇒ diapers [*conf* = 75%]

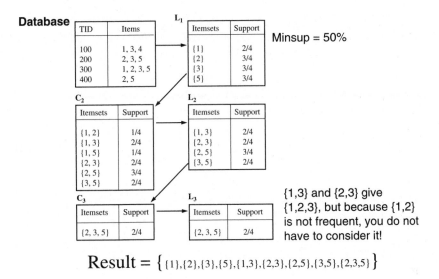

Figure 4.1 The Apriori Algorithm

baby food, diapers ⇒ beer [*conf* = 60%]

beer ⇒ baby food and diapers [*conf* = 50%]

baby food ⇒ diapers and beer [*conf* = 43%]

diapers ⇒ baby food and beer [*conf* = 43%]

If the minconf is set to 70 percent, only the first two association rules will be kept for further analysis.

The Lift Measure

Table 4.3 provides an example from a supermarket transactions database to illustrate the lift measure.

Let's now consider the association rule tea ⇒ coffee. The support of this rule is 100/1,000, or 10 percent. The confidence of the rule is

Table 4.3 The Lift Measure

	Tea	Not Tea	Total
Coffee	150	750	900
Not coffee	50	50	100
Total	200	800	1,000

150/200, or 75 percent. At first sight, this association rule seems very appealing given its high confidence. However, closer inspection reveals that the prior probability of buying coffee equals 900/1,000, or 90 percent. Hence, a customer who buys tea is less likely to buy coffee than a customer about whom we have no information. The lift, also referred to as the *interestingness measure*, takes this into account by incorporating the prior probability of the rule consequent, as follows:

$$Lift(X \rightarrow Y) = \frac{support(X \cup Y)}{support(X) \cdot support(Y)}$$

A lift value less (larger) than 1 indicates a negative (positive) dependence or substitution (complementary) effect. In our example, the lift value equals 0.89, which clearly indicates the expected substitution effect between coffee and tea.

Post Processing Association Rules

Typically, an association rule mining exercise will yield lots of association rules such that post processing will become a key activity. Example steps that can be considered here are:

- Filter out the trivial rules that contain already known patterns (e.g., buying spaghetti and spaghetti sauce). This should be done in collaboration with a business expert.
- Perform a sensitivity analysis by varying the minsup and minconf values. Especially for rare but profitable items (e.g., Rolex watches), it could be interesting to lower the minsup value and find the interesting associations.
- Use appropriate visualization facilities (e.g., OLAP based) to find the unexpected rules that might represent novel and actionable behavior in the data.
- Measure the economic impact (e.g., profit, cost) of the association rules.

Association Rule Extensions

Since the introduction of association rules, various extensions have been proposed. A first extension would be to include item quantities

Figure 4.2 A Product Taxonomy for Association Rule Mining

and/or price. This can be easily accomplished by adding discretized quantitative variables (e.g., three bottles of milk) to the transaction data set and mine the frequent item sets using the Apriori algorithm. Another extension is to also include the absence of items. Also, this can be achieved by adding the absence of items to the transactions data set and again mine using the Apriori algorithm. Finally, multilevel association rules mine association rules at different concept levels of a product taxonomy, as illustrated in Figure 4.2.[2] A similar approach can again be followed here by adding taxonomy information to the transactions data set. Note that different support levels may have to be set for different levels of the product taxonomy.

Applications of Association Rules

The most popular application of association rules is market basket analysis. The aim here is to detect which products or services are frequently purchased together by analyzing market baskets. Finding these associations can have important implications for targeted marketing (e.g., next best offer), product bundling, store and shelf layout, and/or catalog design.

Another popular application is recommender systems. These are the systems adopted by companies such as Amazon and Netflix to give a recommendation based on past purchases and/or browsing behavior.

SEQUENCE RULES

Given a database D of customer transactions, the problem of mining sequential rules is to find the maximal sequences among all sequences that have certain user-specified minimum support and confidence. An example could be a sequence of web page visits in a web analytics setting, as follows:

Home page $\Rightarrow$ Electronics $\Rightarrow$ Cameras and Camcorders $\Rightarrow$ Digital Cameras $\Rightarrow$ Shopping cart $\Rightarrow$ Order confirmation $\Rightarrow$ Return to shopping

It is important to note that a transaction time or sequence field will now be included in the analysis. Whereas association rules are concerned about what items appear together at the same time (intra-transaction patterns), sequence rules are concerned about what items appear at different times (intertransaction patterns). To mine the sequence rules, one can again make use of the *a priori* property because if a sequential pattern of length k is infrequent, its supersets of length $k + 1$ cannot be frequent.

Consider the following example of a transactions data set in a web analytics setting (see Table 4.4). The letters A, B, C, ... refer to web pages.

Table 4.4 Example Transactions Data Set for Sequence Rule Mining

Session ID	Page	Sequence
1	A	1
1	B	2
1	C	3
2	B	1
2	C	2
3	A	1
3	C	2
3	D	3
4	A	1
4	B	2
4	D	3
5	D	1
5	C	1
5	A	1

A sequential version can then be obtained as follows:

Session 1: A, B, C

Session 2: B, C

Session 3: A, C, D

Session 4: A, B, D

Session 5: D, C, A

One can now calculate the support in two different ways. Consider, for example, the sequence rule $A \Rightarrow C$. A first approach would be to calculate the support whereby the consequent can appear in any subsequent stage of the sequence. In this case, the support becomes 2/5 (40%). Another approach would be to only consider sessions in which the consequent appears right after the antecedent. In this case, the support becomes 1/5 (20%). A similar reasoning can now be followed for the confidence, which can then be 2/4 (50%) or 1/4 (25%), respectively.

Remember that the confidence of a rule $A_1 \Rightarrow A_2$ is defined as the probability $P(A_2|A_1) = \text{support}(A_1 \cup A_2)/\text{support}(A_1)$. For a rule with multiple items, $A_1 \Rightarrow A_2 \Rightarrow \dots A_{n-1} \Rightarrow A_n$, the confidence is defined as $P(A_n|A_1, A_2, \dots, A_{n-1})$, or $\text{support}(A_1 \cup A_2 \cup \dots \cup A_{n-1} \cup A_n)/\text{support}$ $(A_1 \cup A_2 \cup \dots \cup A_{n-1})$.

SEGMENTATION

The aim of segmentation is to split up a set of customer observations into segments such that the homogeneity within a segment is maximized (cohesive) and the heterogeneity between segments is maximized (separated). Popular applications include:

- Understanding a customer population (e.g., targeted marketing or advertising [mass customization])
- Efficiently allocating marketing resources
- Differentiating between brands in a portfolio
- Identifying the most profitable customers
- Identifying shopping patterns
- Identifying the need for new products

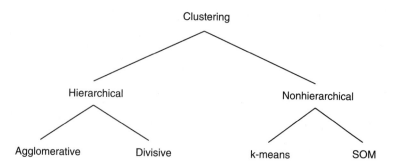

Figure 4.3 Hierarchical versus Nonhierarchical Clustering Techniques

Various types of clustering data can be used, such as demographic, lifestyle, attitudinal, behavioral, RFM, acquisitional, social network, and so on.

Clustering techniques can be categorized as either hierarchical or nonhierarchical (see Figure 4.3).

Hierarchical Clustering

In what follows, we will first discuss hierarchical clustering. Divisive hierarchical clustering starts from the whole data set in one cluster, and then breaks this up in each time smaller clusters until one observation per cluster remains (right to left in Figure 4.4). Agglomerative clustering works the other way around, starting from all

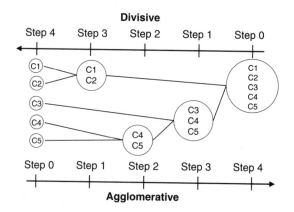

Figure 4.4 Divisive versus Agglomerative Hierarchical Clustering

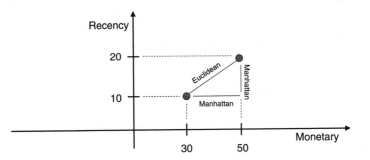

Figure 4.5 Euclidean versus Manhattan Distance

observations in one cluster and continuing to merge the ones that are most similar until all observations make up one big cluster (left to right in Figure 4.4).

In order to decide on the merger or splitting, a similarity rule is needed. Examples of popular similarity rules are the Euclidean distance and Manhattan (city block) distance. For the example in Figure 4.5, both are calculated as follows:

$$Euclidean: \sqrt{(50-30)^2 + (20-10)^2} = 22$$
$$Manhattan: |50-30| + |20-10| = 30$$

It is obvious that the Euclidean distance will always be shorter than the Manhattan distance.

Various schemes can now be adopted to calculate the distance between two clusters (see Figure 4.6). The single linkage method

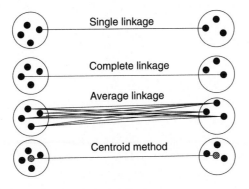

Figure 4.6 Calculating Distances between Clusters

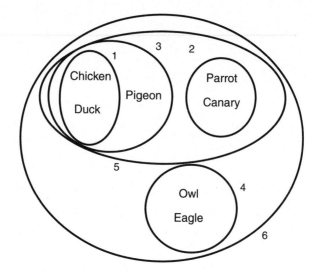

Figure 4.7 Example for Clustering Birds
The numbers indicate the clustering steps.

defines the distance between two clusters as the shortest possible distance, or the distance between the two most similar objects. The complete linkage method defines the distance between two clusters as the biggest distance, or the distance between the two most dissimilar objects. The average linkage method calculates the average of all possible distances. The centroid method calculates the distance between the centroids of both clusters. Finally, Ward's method merges the pair of clusters that leads to the minimum increase in total within-cluster variance after merging.

In order to decide on the optimal number of clusters, one could use a dendrogram or scree plot. A dendrogram is a tree-like diagram that records the sequences of merges. The vertical (or horizontal scale) then gives the distance between two clusters amalgamated. One can then cut the dendrogram at the desired level to find the optimal clustering. This is illustrated in Figure 4.7 and Figure 4.8 for a birds clustering example. A scree plot is a plot of the distance at which clusters are merged. The elbow point then indicates the optimal clustering. This is illustrated in Figure 4.9.

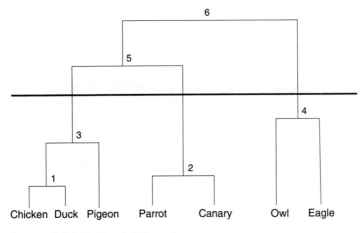

Figure 4.8 Dendrogram for Birds Example
The black line indicates the optimal clustering.

K-Means Clustering

K-means clustering is a nonhierarchical procedure that works along the following steps:

1. Select k observations as initial cluster centroids (seeds).
2. Assign each observation to the cluster that has the closest centroid (for example, in Euclidean sense).
3. When all observations have been assigned, recalculate the positions of the k centroids.
4. Repeat until the cluster centroids no longer change.

A key requirement here is that the number of clusters, k, needs to be specified before the start of the analysis. It is also advised to try out different seeds to verify the stability of the clustering solution.

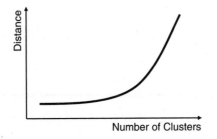

Figure 4.9 Scree Plot for Clustering

Self-Organizing Maps

A self-organizing map (SOM) is an unsupervised learning algorithm that allows you to visualize and cluster high-dimensional data on a low-dimensional grid of neurons.[3] An SOM is a feedforward neural network with two layers. The neurons from the output layer are usually ordered in a two-dimensional rectangular or hexagonal grid (see Figure 4.10). For the former, every neuron has at most eight neighbors, whereas for the latter every neuron has at most six neighbors.

Each input is connected to all neurons in the output layer with weights $w = [w_1, ..., w_N]$, with N the number of variables. All weights are randomly initialized. When a training vector x is presented, the weight vector w_c of each neuron c is compared with x, using, for example, the Euclidean distance metric (beware to standardize the data first):

$$d(x, w_c) = \sqrt{\sum_{i=1}^{N} (x_i - w_{ci})^2}$$

The neuron that is most similar to x in Euclidean sense is called the best matching unit (BMU). The weight vector of the BMU and its neighbors in the grid are then adapted using the following learning rule:

$$w_i(t+1) = w_i(t+1) + h_{ci}(t)\left[x(t) - w_i(t)\right]$$

whereby t represents the time index during training and $h_{ci}(t)$ defines the neighborhood of the BMU c, specifying the region of influence. The

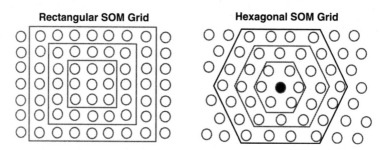

Figure 4.10   Rectangular versus Hexagonal SOM Grid

neighborhood function $h_{ci}(t)$ should be a nonincreasing function of time and the distance from the BMU. Some popular choices are:

$$h_{ci}(t) = \alpha(t)\exp\left(-\frac{\left\|r_c - r_i\right\|^2}{2\sigma^2(t)}\right)$$

$$h_{ci}(t) = \alpha(t) \text{ if } \left\|r_c - r_i\right\|^2 \leq \text{threshold}, 0 \text{ otherwise,}$$

whereby r_c and r_i represent the location of the BMU and neuron i on the map, $\sigma^2(t)$ represents the decreasing radius, and $0 \leq \alpha(t) \leq 1$, the learning rate (e.g., $\alpha(t) = A/(t + B)$, $\alpha(t) = \exp(-At)$). The decreasing learning rate and radius will give a stable map after a certain amount of training. Training is stopped when the BMUs remain stable, or after a fixed number of iterations (e.g., 500 times the number of SOM neurons). The neurons will then move more and more toward the input observations and interesting segments will emerge.

SOMs can be visualized by means of a U-matrix or component plane.

- A U (unified distance)-matrix essentially superimposes a height Z dimension on top of each neuron visualizing the average distance between the neuron and its neighbors, whereby typically dark colors indicate a large distance and can be interpreted as cluster boundaries.
- A component plane visualizes the weights between each specific input variable and its output neurons, and as such provides a visual overview of the relative contribution of each input attribute to the output neurons.

Figure 4.11 provides an SOM example for clustering countries based on a corruption perception index (CPI). This is a score between 0 (highly corrupt) and 10 (highly clean) assigned to each country in the world. The CPI is combined with demographic and macroeconomic information for the years 1996, 2000, and 2004. Upper case countries (e.g., BEL) denote the situation in 2004, lowercase (e.g., bel) in 2000, and sentence case (e.g., Bel) in 1996. It can be seen that many of the European countries are situated in the upper right corner of the map.

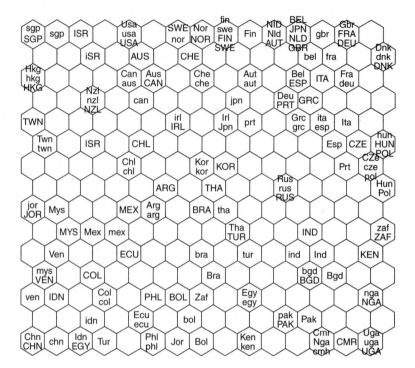

Figure 4.11 Clustering Countries Using SOMs

Figure 4.12 provides the component plane for literacy whereby darker regions score worse on literacy. Figure 4.13 provides the component plane for political rights whereby darker regions correspond to better political rights. It can be seen that many of the European countries score good on both literacy and political rights.

SOMs are a very handy tool for clustering high-dimensional data sets because of the visualization facilities. However, since there is no real objective function to minimize, it is harder to compare various SOM solutions against each other. Also, experimental evaluation and expert interpretation are needed to decide on the optimal size of the SOM. Unlike k-means clustering, an SOM does not force the number of clusters to be equal to the number of output neurons.

Using and Interpreting Clustering Solutions

In order to use a clustering scheme, one can assign new observations to the cluster for which the centroid is closest (e.g., in Euclidean or

Figure 4.12   Component Plane for Literacy

Figure 4.13   Component Plane for Political Rights

Manhattan sense). To facilitate the interpretation of a clustering solution, one could do the following:

- Compare cluster averages with population averages for all variables using histograms, for example.
- Build a decision tree with the cluster ID as the target and the clustering variables as the inputs (can also be used to assign new observations to clusters).

It is also important to check cluster stability by running different clustering techniques on different samples with different parameter settings and check the robustness of the solution.

NOTES

1. R. Agrawal, T. Imielinski, and A. Swami, "Mining Association Rules between Sets of Items in Massive Databases," in *Proceedings of the ACM SIGMOD International Conference on Management of Data* (Washington, DC, ACM, 1993).

2. R. Srikant and R. Agrawal, "Mining Generalized Association Rules," in *Proceedings of the 1995 International Conference on Very Large Data Bases* (Zurich, 1995).

3. T. Kohonen, "Self-Organized Formation of Topologically Correct Feature Maps," *Biological Cybernetics* 43 (1982): 59–69; J. Huysmans et al., "Using Self Organizing Maps for Credit Scoring," Special issue on Intelligent Information Systems for Financial Engineering, Expert Systems With Applications, 30, no. 3 (2006): 479–487; A. Seret et al., "A New SOM-Based Method for Profile Generation: Theory and an Application in Direct Marketing," *European Journal of Operational Research* 220, no. 1 (2012): 199–209.

CHAPTER 5

Survival Analysis

Survival analysis is a set of statistical techniques focusing on the occurrence and timing of events.[1] As the name suggests, it originates from a medical context where it was used to study survival times of patients that had received certain treatments. In fact, many classification analytics problems we have discussed before also have a time aspect included, which can be analyzed using survival analysis techniques. Some examples are:[2]

- Predict when customers churn
- Predict when customers make their next purchase
- Predict when customers default
- Predict when customers pay off their loan early
- Predict when customer will visit a website next

Two typical problems complicate the usage of classical statistical techniques such as linear regression. A first key problem is censoring. Censoring refers to the fact that the target time variable is not always known because not all customers may have undergone the event yet at the time of the analysis. Consider, for example, the example depicted in Figure 5.1. At time T, Laura and John have not churned yet and thus have no value for the target time indicator. The only information available is that they will churn at some later date after T. Note also that Sophie is censored at the time she moved to Australia. In fact, these are all examples of right censoring. An observation on a variable T is right censored if all you know about T is that it is greater than some value c.

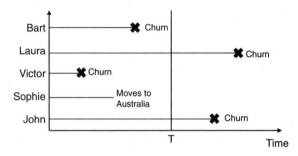

Figure 5.1 Example of Right Censoring for Churn Prediction

Likewise, an observation on a variable T is left censored if all you know about T is that it is smaller than some value c. An example here could be a study investigating smoking behavior and some participants at age 18 already began smoking but can no longer remember the exact date. Interval censoring means the only information available on T is that it belongs to some interval $a < T < b$. Returning to the previous smoking example, one could be more precise and say $14 < T < 18$. Censoring occurs because many databases only contain current or rather recent customers for whom the behavior has not yet been completely observed, or because of database errors when, for example, the event dates are missing. Using classical statistical analysis techniques such as linear regression, the censored observations would have to be left out from the analysis, since they have no value for the target time variable. However, with survival analysis, the partial information available for the censored observations giving either a lower and/or an upper bound on the timing of the event will be included in the estimation.

Time-varying covariates are variables that change value during the course of the study. Examples are account balance, income, and credit scores. Survival analysis techniques will be able to accommodate this in the model formulation, as will be discussed in what follows.

SURVIVAL ANALYSIS MEASUREMENTS

A first important concept is the event time distribution defined as a continuous probability distribution, as follows:

$$f(t) = \lim_{\Delta t \to 0} \frac{P(t \le T < t + \Delta T)}{\Delta t}$$

The corresponding cumulative event time distribution is then defined as follows:

$$F(t) = P(T \leq t) = \int_0^t f(u)\,du$$

Closely related is the survival function:

$$S(t) = 1 - F(t) = P(T > t) = \int_t^\infty f(u)\,du$$

$S(t)$ is a monotonically decreasing function with $S(0) = 1$ and $S(\infty) = 0$. The following relationships hold:

$$f(t) = \frac{dF(t)}{dt} = -\frac{dS(t)}{dt}$$

Figure 5.2 provides an example of a discrete event time distribution, with the corresponding cumulative event time and survival distribution depicted in Figure 5.3.

Another important measure in survival analysis is the hazard function, defined as follows:

$$h(t) = \lim_{\Delta t \to 0} \frac{P(t \leq T < t + \Delta T \mid T \geq t)}{\Delta t}$$

The hazard function tries to quantify the instantaneous risk that an event will occur at time t, given that the individual has survived up to time t. Hence, it tries to measure the risk of the event occurring at time point t. The hazard function is closely related to the event time

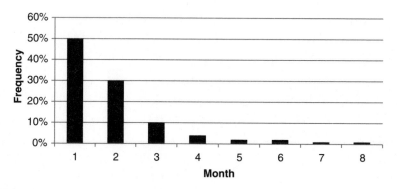

Figure 5.2 Example of a Discrete Event Time Distribution

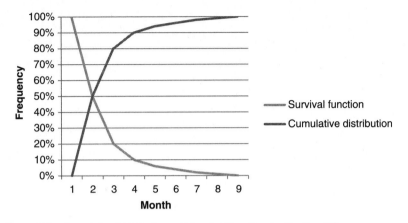

Figure 5.3 Cumulative Distribution and Survival Function for the Event Time Distribution in Figure 5.2

distribution up to the conditioning on $T \geq t$. That is why it is often also referred to as a *conditional density*.

Figure 5.4 provides some examples of hazard shapes, as follows:

- Constant hazard, whereby the risk remains the same at all times.
- Increasing hazard, reflecting an aging effect.
- Decreasing hazard, reflecting a curing effect.
- Convex bathtub shape, which is typically the case when studying human mortality, since mortality declines after birth and infancy, remains low for a while, and increases with elder years. It is also a property of some mechanical systems to either fail soon after operation, or much later, as the system ages.

The probability density function $f(t)$, survivor function $S(t)$, and the hazard function $h(t)$ are mathematically equivalent ways of describing a continuous probability distribution with the following relationships:

$$h(t) = \frac{f(t)}{S(t)}$$

$$h(t) = -\frac{dlogS(t)}{dt}$$

$$S(t) = \exp\left(-\int_0^t h(u)\,du\right)$$

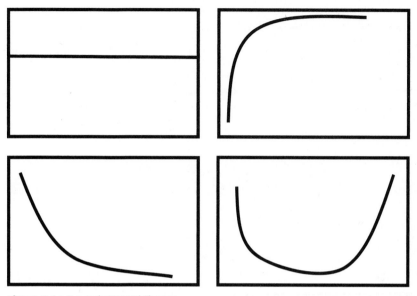

Figure 5.4 Example Hazard Shapes

KAPLAN MEIER ANALYSIS

A first type of survival analysis is Kaplan Meier (KM) analysis, which is also known as the product limit estimator or nonparametric maximum likelihood estimator for $S(t)$. If no censoring is available in the data set, the KM estimator for $S(t)$ is just the sample proportion with event times greater than t. If censoring is present, the KM estimator starts with ordering the event times in ascending order $t_1 < t_2 < \ldots < t_k$. At each time t_j, there are n_j individuals who are at risk of the event. At risk means that they have not undergone the event, nor have they been censored prior to t_j. Let d_j be the number of individuals who die (e.g., churn, respond, default) at t_j. The KM estimator is then defined as follows:

$$\hat{S}(t) = \prod_{j:t_j \leq t}\left(1 - \frac{d_j}{n_j}\right) = \hat{S}(t-1)\cdot\left(1 - \frac{d_t}{n_t}\right) = \hat{S}(t-1)\cdot(1 - h(t))$$

for $t_1 \leq t \leq t_k$. The intuition of the KM estimator is very straightforward because it basically states that in order to survive time t, one must survive time $t - 1$ and cannot die during time t.

Figure 5.5 gives an example of Kaplan Meier analysis for churn prediction.

Customer	Time of Churn or Censoring	Churn or Censored
C1	6	Churn
C2	3	Censored
C3	12	Churn
C4	15	Censored
C5	18	Censored
C6	12	Churn
C7	3	Churn
C8	12	Churn
C9	9	Censored
C10	15	Churn

Time	Customers at Risk at t (n_t)	Customers Churned at t (d_t)	Customers Censored at t	S(t)
0	10	0	0	1
3	10	1	1	0.9
6	8	1	0	0.9* 7/8 = 0.79
9	7	0	1	0.79* 7/7 = 0.79
12	6	3	0	0.79* 3/6 = 0.39
15	3	1	1	0.39* 2/3 = 0.26
18	1	0	1	0.26* 1/1 = 0.26

Figure 5.5 Kaplan Meier Example

If there are many unique event times, the KM estimator can be adjusted by using the life table (also known as *actuarial*) method to group event times into intervals as follows:

$$\hat{S}(t) = \prod_{j:t_j \le t}\left[1 - \frac{d_j}{n_j - c_j/2}\right]$$

which basically assumes that censoring occurs uniformly across the time interval, such that the average number at risk equals $(n_j + (n_j - c_j))/2$ or $n_j - c_j/2$.

Kaplan Meier analysis can also be extended with hypothesis testing to see whether the survival curves of different groups (e.g., men versus women, employed versus unemployed) are statistically different. Popular test statistics here are the log-rank test (also known as the *Mantel-Haenzel test*), the Wilcoxon test, and the likelihood ratio statistic, which are all readily available in any commercial analytics software.

KM analysis is a good way to start doing some exploratory survival analysis. However, it would be nice to be able to also build predictive survival analysis models that take into account customer heterogeneity by including predictive variables or covariates.

PARAMETRIC SURVIVAL ANALYSIS

As the name suggests, parametric survival analysis models assume a parametric shape for the event time distribution. A first popular choice is an exponential distribution, defined as follows:

$$f(t) = \lambda e^{-\lambda t}$$

Using the relationships defined earlier, the survival function then becomes:

$$S(t) = e^{-\lambda t}$$

and the hazard rate

$$h(t) = \frac{f(t)}{S(t)} = \lambda$$

It is worth noting that the hazard rate is independent of time such that the risk always remains the same. This is often referred to as the *memoryless property* of an exponential distribution. Figure 5.6 shows an example of an exponential event time distribution together with its cumulative distribution and hazard function.

When taking into account covariates, the model becomes:

$$\log(h(t, x_i)) = \mu + \beta_1 x_{i1} + \beta_2 x_{i2} + \cdots \beta_N x_{iN}$$

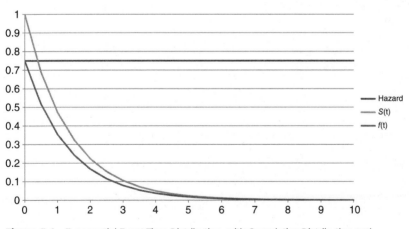

Figure 5.6 Exponential Event Time Distribution, with Cumulative Distribution and Hazard Function

Note that the logarithmic transform is used here to make sure that the hazard rate is always positive.

The Weibull distribution is another popular choice for a parametric survival analysis model. It is defined as follows:

$$f(t) = \kappa\rho(\rho t)^{\kappa-1}\exp[-(\rho t)^{\kappa}]$$

The survival function then becomes:

$$S(t) = \exp[-(\rho t)^{\kappa}]$$

and the hazard rate

$$h(t) = \frac{f(t)}{S(t)} = \kappa\rho(\rho t)^{\kappa-1}$$

Note that in this case the hazard rate does depend on time and can be either increasing or decreasing (depending upon κ and ρ).

When including covariates, the model becomes:

$$\log(h(t, x_i)) = \mu + \alpha\log(t) + \beta_1 x_{i1} + \beta_2 x_{i2} + \cdots \beta_N x_{iN}$$

Other popular choices for the event time distribution are the gamma, log-logistic, and log-normal distribution.[3]

Parametric survival analysis models are typically estimated using maximum likelihood procedures. In case of no censored observations, the likelihood function becomes:

$$L = \prod_{i=1}^{n} f(t_i)$$

When censoring is present, the likelihood function becomes:

$$L = \prod_{i=1}^{n} f(t_i)^{\delta_i} S(t_i)^{1-\delta_i}$$

whereby δ_i equals 0 if observation i is censored, and 1 if the observation dies at time t_i. It is important to note here that the censored observations do enter the likelihood function and, as such, have an impact on the estimates. For example, for the exponential distribution, the likelihood function becomes:

$$L = \prod_{i=1}^{n} [\lambda e^{-\lambda t_i}]^{\delta_i} [e^{-\lambda t_i}]^{1-\delta_i}$$

This maximum likelihood function is then typically optimized by further taking the logarithm and then using a Newton Raphson optimization procedure.

A key question concerns the appropriate event time distribution for a given set of survival data. This question can be answered both in a graphical and a statistical way.

In order to solve it graphically, we can start from the following relationships:

$$h(t) = -\frac{d \log S(t)}{dt}$$

or

$$-\log(S(t)) = \int_0^t h(u) \, du$$

Because of this relationship, the log survivor function is commonly referred to as the *cumulative hazard function,* denoted as $\Lambda(t)$. It can be interpreted as the sum of the risks that are faced when going from time 0 to time t. If the survival times are exponentially distributed, then the hazard is constant, $h(t) = \lambda$, hence $\Lambda(t) = \lambda t$ and a plot of $-\log(S(t))$ versus t should yield a straight line through the origin at 0. Similarly, it can be shown that if the survival times are Weibull distributed, then a plot of $\log(-\log(S(t))$ versus $\log(t)$ should yield a straight line (not through the origin) with a slope of κ. These plots can typically be asked for in any commercial analytics software implementing survival analysis. Note, however, that this graphical method is not a very precise method because the lines will never be perfectly linear or go through the origin.

A more precise method for testing the appropriate event time distribution is a likelihood ratio test. In fact, the likelihood ratio test can be used to compare models if one model is a special case of another (nested models). Consider the following generalized gamma distribution:

$$f(t) = \frac{\beta}{\Gamma(t)\theta}\left(\frac{t}{\theta}\right)^{k\beta-1} e^{-\left(\frac{t}{\theta}\right)^{\beta}}$$

Let's now use the following shortcut notations: $\sigma = \dfrac{1}{\beta\sqrt{k}}$ and $\delta = \dfrac{1}{\sqrt{k}}$, then the Weibull, exponential, standard gamma, and log-normal model are all special versions of the generalized gamma model, as follows:

- $\sigma = \delta$: standard gamma
- $\delta = 1$: Weibull
- $\sigma = \delta = 1$: exponential
- $\delta = 0$: log-normal

Let L_{full} now be the likelihood of the full model (e.g., generalized gamma) and L_{red} be the likelihood of the reduced (specialized) model (e.g., exponential). The likelihood ratio test statistic then becomes:

$$-2\log\left(\frac{L_{red}}{L_{full}}\right) \sim \chi^2(k)$$

whereby the degrees of freedom k depends on the number of parameters that need to be set to go from the full model to the reduced model. In other words, it is set as follows:

- Exponential versus Weibull: one degree of freedom
- Exponential versus standard gamma: one degree of freedom
- Exponential versus generalized gamma: two degrees of freedom
- Weibull versus generalized gamma: one degree of freedom
- Log-normal versus generalized gamma: one degree of freedom
- Standard gamma versus generalized gamma: one degree of freedom

The χ^2-test statistic can then be calculated together with the corresponding p-value and a decision can be made about what is the most appropriate event time distribution.

PROPORTIONAL HAZARDS REGRESSION

The proportional hazards model is formulated as follows:

$$h(t, x_i) = h_0(t)\exp(\beta_1 x_{i1} + \beta_2 x_{i2} + \cdots + \beta_N x_{iN})$$

so the hazard of an individual i with characteristics x_i at time t is the product of a baseline hazard function $h_0(t)$ and a linear function of a set of fixed covariates, which is exponentiated. In fact, $h_0(t)$ can be considered as the hazard for an individual with all covariates equal to 0. Note that if a variable j increases with one unit and all other variables keep their values (*ceteris paribus*), then the hazards for all t increase with $\exp(\beta_j)$, which is called the *hazard ratio* (HR). If $\beta_j > 0$ then HR > 1, $\beta_j < 0$ then HR < 1; $\beta_j = 0$ then HR $= 1$. This is one of the most popular models for doing survival analysis.

The name *proportional hazards* stems from the fact that the hazard of any individual is a fixed proportion of the hazard of any other individual.

$$\frac{h_i(t)}{h_j(t)} = \exp(\beta_1(x_{i1} - x_{j1}) + \beta_1(x_{i2} - x_{j2}) + \cdots + \beta_n(x_{iN} - x_{jN})).$$

Hence, the subjects most at risk at any one time remain the subjects most at risk at any one other time (see also Figure 5.7).

Taking logarithms from the original proportional hazards model gives:

$$\log h(t, x_i) = \alpha(t) + \beta_1 x_{i1} + \beta_2 x_{i2} + \cdots + \beta_N x_{iN}$$

Note that if one chooses $\alpha(t) = \alpha$, one gets the exponential model, whereas if $\alpha(t) = \alpha \log(t)$, the Weibull model is obtained. A nice property of the proportional hazards model is that, using the idea of partial likelihood, the βs can be estimated without having to explicitly specify the baseline hazard function $h_0(t)$.[4] This is useful if one is only interested in analyzing the impact of the covariates on the hazard rates and/or survival probabilities. However, if one wants to make predictions

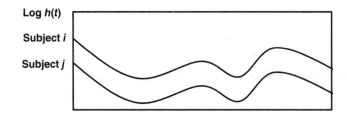

Figure 5.7   The Proportional Hazards Model

with the proportional hazards model, the baseline hazard needs to be explicitly specified.

The survival function that comes with the proportional hazards model looks like this:

$$S(t, x_i) = \exp\left[-\int_0^t h_0(u)\exp(\beta_1 x_{i1} + \beta_2 x_{i2} + \cdots + \beta_N x_{iN})du \right], \text{ or}$$

$$S(t, x_i) = S_0(t)^{\exp(\beta_1 x_{i1} + \beta_2 x_{i2} + \cdots + \beta_N x_{iN})}, \text{ with}$$

$$S_0(t) = \exp\left(-\int_0^t h_0(u)\,du \right)$$

$S_0(t)$ is referred to as the *baseline survivor function*, that is, the survivor function for an individual whose covariates are all 0. Note that if a variable j increases with one unit (*ceteris paribus*), the survival probabilities are raised to the power $\exp(\beta_j)$, which is the hazard ratio (HR).

EXTENSIONS OF SURVIVAL ANALYSIS MODELS

A first extension of the models we previously discussed is the inclusion of time-varying covariates. These are variables that change value throughout the course of the study. The model then becomes:

$$h(t, x_i) = h_0(t)\exp(\beta_1 x_{i1}(t) + \beta_2 x_{i2}(t) + \cdots + \beta_N x_{iN}(t))$$

Note that the proportional hazards assumption here no longer holds because the time-varying covariates may change at different rates for different subjects, so the ratios of their hazards will not remain constant. One could also let the β parameters vary in time, as follows:

$$h(t, x_i) = h_0(t)\exp(\beta_1(t)x_{i1}(t) + \beta_2(t)x_{i2}(t) + \cdots + \beta_N(t)x_{iN}(t))$$

The partial likelihood estimation method referred to earlier can easily be extended to accommodate these changes in the model formulation, such that the coefficients can also be estimated without explicitly specifying the baseline hazard $h_0(t)$.

Another extension is the idea of competing risks.[5] Often, an observation can experience any of k competing events. In medicine, customers may die because of cancer or ageing. In a bank setting, a customer can default, pay off early, or churn at a given time. As long as a customer has not undergone any of the events, he or she remains at risk for any event. Once a customer has undergone the event, he or she is no longer included in the population at risk for any of the other risk groups, hence he or she becomes censored for the other risks.

Although the ideas of time-varying covariates and competing risks seem attractive at first sight, the number of successful business applications of both remains very limited, due to the extra complexity introduced in the model(s).

EVALUATING SURVIVAL ANALYSIS MODELS

A survival analysis model can be evaluated by first considering the statistical significance of both the model as a whole and the individual covariates. (Remember: Significant covariates have low p-values.) One could also predict the time of the event when the survival curve $S(t)$ drops below 0,50 and compare this with the real event time. Another option is to take a snapshot of the survival probabilities at a specific time t (e.g., 12 months), compare this with the event time indicator, and calculate the corresponding ROC curve and its area beneath. The AUC will then indicate how well the model ranks the observations for a specific timestamp t. Finally, one could also evaluate the interpretability of the survival analysis model by using univariate sign checks on the covariates and seeing whether they correspond to business expert knowledge.

The survival analysis models we have discussed in this chapter are classical statistical models. Hence, some important drawbacks are that the functional relationship remains linear or some mild extension thereof, interaction and nonlinear terms have to be specified ad hoc, extreme hazards may occur for outlying observations, and there is the assumption of proportional hazards that may not always be the case. Other methods have been described in the literature to tackle these shortcomings, based on, for example, splines and neural networks.[6]

NOTES

1. P. D. Allison, *Survival Analysis Using the SAS System* (SAS Institute Inc., Cary, NC, US, 1995); D. R. Cox, "Regression Models and Life Tables," *Journal of the Royal Statistical Society*, series B (1972); D. R. Cox and D. Oakes, *Analysis of Survival Data* (Chapman

and Hall, 1984); D. Kalbfleisch and R. L. Prentice, *The Statistical Analysis of Failure Time Data* (New York: Wiley, 2003).

2. J. Banasik, J. N. Crook, and L. C. Thomas, "Not If but When Borrowers Will Default," *Journal of the Operational Research Society* 50, no. 12 (1999): 1185–1190; L. C. Thomas and M. Stepanova, "Survival Analysis Methods for Personal Loan Data," *Operations Research* 50 (2002): 277–289.

3. P. D. Allison, *Survival Analysis using the SAS System* (SAS Institute Inc., Cary, NC, US, 1995).

4. P. D. Allison, *Survival Analysis Using the SAS System* (SAS Institute Inc., Cary, NC, US,1995); D. R. Cox, "Regression Models and Life Tables," *Journal of the Royal Statistical Society*, series B (1972); D. R. Cox and D. Oakes, *Analysis of Survival Data* (Chapman and Hall, 1984); D. Kalbfleisch and R. L. Prentice, *The Statistical Analysis of Failure Time Data* (New York: Wiley, 2003).

5. M. J. Crowder, *Classical Competing Risks* (London: Chapman and Hall, 2001).

6. B. Baesens et al., "Neural Network Survival Analysis for Personal Loan Data." Special issue, *Journal of the Operational Research Society* 59, no. 9 (2005): 1089–1098.

CHAPTER 6

Social Network Analytics

M any types of social networks exist. The most popular are undoubtedly Facebook, Twitter, Google+, and LinkedIn. However, social networks are more than that. It could be any set of nodes (also referred to as *vertices*) connected by edges in a particular business setting. Examples of social networks could be:

- Web pages connected by hyperlinks
- Email traffic between people
- Research papers connected by citations
- Telephone calls between customers of a telco provider
- Banks connected by liquidity dependencies
- Spread of illness between patients

These examples clearly illustrate that social network analytics can be applied in a wide variety of different settings.

SOCIAL NETWORK DEFINITIONS

A social network consists of both nodes (vertices) and edges. Both need to be clearly defined at the outset of the analysis. A node (vertex) could be defined as a customer (private/professional), household/ family, patient, doctor, paper, author, terrorist, web page, and so forth. An edge can be defined as a friend relationship, a call, transmission

119

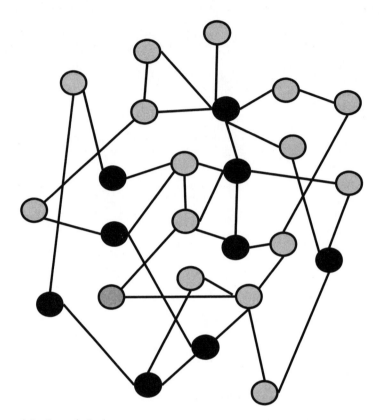

Figure 6.1 Example Sociogram

of a disease, reference, and so on. Note that the edges can also be weighted based on interaction frequency, importance of information exchange, intimacy, and emotional intensity. For example, in a churn prediction setting, the edge can be weighted according to the time two customers called each other during a specific period. Social networks can be represented as a sociogram. This is illustrated in Figure 6.1, whereby the color of the nodes corresponds to a specific status (e.g., churner or nonchurner).

Sociograms are good for small-scale networks. For larger-scale networks, the network will typically be represented as a matrix, as illustrated in Table 6.1. These matrices will be symmetrical and typically very sparse (with lots of zeros). The matrix can also contain the weights in case of weighted connections.

Table 6.1 Matrix Representation of a Social Network

	C1	C2	C3	C4
C1	—	1	1	0
C2	1	—	0	1
C3	1	0	—	0
C4	0	1	0	—

SOCIAL NETWORK METRICS

A social network can be characterized by various social network metrics. The most important centrality measures are depicted in Table 6.2. Assume a network with g nodes n_i, $i = 1, ..., g$. g_{jk} represents the number of geodesics from node j to node k, whereas $g_{jk}(n_i)$ represents the number of geodesics from node j to node k passing through node n_i. The formulas each time calculate the metric for node n_i.

These metrics can now be illustrated with the well-known Kite network depicted in Figure 6.2.

Table 6.3 reports the centrality measures for the Kite network. Based on degree, Diane has the most connections. She works as a

Table 6.2 Network Centrality Measures

Geodesic	Shortest path between two nodes in the network	
Degree	Number of connections of a node (in- versus out-degree if the connections are directed)	
Closeness	The average distance of a node to all other nodes in the network (reciprocal of farness)	$\left[\dfrac{\sum_{j=1}^{g} d(n_i n_j)}{g} \right]^{-1}$
Betweenness	Counts the number of times a node or connection lies on the shortest path between any two nodes in the network	$\sum_{j<k} \dfrac{g_{jk}(n_i)}{g_{jk}}$
Graph theoretic center	The node with the smallest maximum distance to all other nodes in the network	

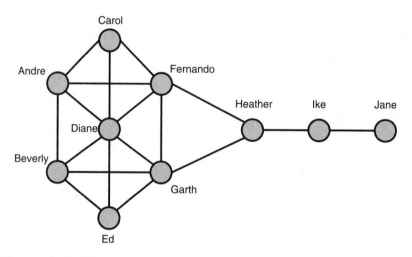

Figure 6.2 The Kite Network

connector or hub. Note, however, that she only connects those already connected to each other. Fernando and Garth are the closest to all others. They are the best positioned to communicate messages that need to flow quickly through to all other nodes in the network. Heather has the highest betweenness. She sits in between two important communities (Ike and Jane versus the rest). She plays a broker role between both communities but is also a single point of failure. Note that the betweenness measure is often used for community

Table 6.3 Centrality Measures for the Kite Network

Degree		Closeness		Betweenness	
6	Diane	0.64	Fernando	14	Heather
5	Fernando	0.64	Garth	8.33	Fernando
5	Garth	0.6	Diane	8.33	Garth
4	Andre	0.6	Heather	8	Ike
4	Beverly	0.53	Andre	3.67	Diane
3	Carol	0.53	Beverly	0.83	Andre
3	Ed	0.5	Carol	0.83	Beverly
3	Heather	0.5	Ed	0	Carol
2	Ike	0.43	Ike	0	Ed
1	Jane	0.31	Jane	0	Jane

mining. A popular technique here is the Girvan-Newman algorithm, which works as follows:[1]

1. The betweenness of all existing edges in the network is calculated first.
2. The edge with the highest betweenness is removed.
3. The betweenness of all edges affected by the removal is recalculated.
4. Steps 2 and 3 are repeated until no edges remain.

The result of this procedure is essentially a dendrogram, which can then be used to decide on the optimal number of communities.

SOCIAL NETWORK LEARNING

In social network learning, the goal is within-network classification to compute the marginal class membership probability of a particular node given the other nodes in the network. Various important challenges arise when learning in social networks. A first key challenge is that the data are not independent and identically distributed (IID), an assumption often made in classical statistical models (e.g., linear and logistic regression). The correlational behavior between nodes implies that the class membership of one node might influence the class membership of a related node. Next, it is not easy to come up with a separation into a training set for model development and a test set for model validation, since the whole network is interconnected and cannot just be cut into two parts. Also, there is a strong need for collective inferencing procedures because inferences about nodes can mutually influence one another. Moreover, many networks are huge in scale (e.g., a call graph from a telco provider), and efficient computational procedures need to be developed to do the learning.[2] Finally, one should not forget the traditional way of doing analytics using only node-specific information because this can still prove to be very valuable information for prediction as well.

Given the above remarks, a social network learner will usually consist of the following components:[3]

- A local model: This is a model using only node-specific characteristics, typically estimated using a classical predictive analytics model (e.g., logistic regression, decision tree).

- A network model: This is a model that will make use of the connections in the network to do the inferencing.

- A collective inferencing procedure: This is a procedure to determine how the unknown nodes are estimated together, hereby influencing each other.

In order to facilitate the computations, one often makes use of the Markov property, stating that the class of a node in the network only depends on the class of its direct neighbors (and not of the neighbors of the neighbors). Although this assumption may seem limiting at first sight, empirical evaluation has demonstrated that it is a reasonable assumption to be made.

RELATIONAL NEIGHBOR CLASSIFIER

The relational neighbor classifier makes use of the homophily assumption, which states that connected nodes have a propensity to belong to the same class. This idea is also referred to as *guilt by association*. If two nodes are associated, they tend to exhibit similar behavior. The posterior class probability for node n to belong to class c is then calculated as follows:

$$P(c|n) = \frac{1}{Z} \sum_{\{n_j \in Neighborhood_n | class(n_j)=c\}} w(n,n_j)$$

whereby $Neighborhood_n$ represents the neighborhood of node n, $w(n,n_j)$ the weight of the connection between n and n_j, and Z is a normalization factor to make sure all probabilities sum to one.

For example, consider the network depicted in Figure 6.3, whereby C and NC represent churner and nonchurner nodes, respectively.

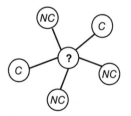

Figure 6.3 Example Social Network for Relational Neighbor Classifier

The calculations then become:

$$P(C|?) = 1/Z(1+1)$$

$$P(NC|?) = 1/Z(1+1+1)$$

Since both probabilities have to sum to 1, Z equals 5, so the probabilities become:

$$P(C|?) = 2/5$$

$$P(NC|?) = 3/5$$

PROBABILISTIC RELATIONAL NEIGHBOR CLASSIFIER

The probabilistic relational neighbor classifier is a straightforward extension of the relational neighbor classifier, whereby the posterior class probability for node n to belong to class c is calculated as follows:

$$P(c|n) = \frac{1}{Z} \sum_{\{n_j \in Neighborhood_n\}} w(n, n_j) P(c|n_j)$$

Note that the summation now ranges over the entire neighborhood of nodes. The probabilities $P(c|n_j)$ can be the result of a local model or of a previously applied network model. Consider the network of Figure 6.4.

The calculations then become:

$$P(C|?) = 1/Z(0.25 + 0.80 + 0.10 + 0.20 + 0.90) = 2.25/Z$$

$$P(NC|?) = 1/Z(0.75 + 0.20 + 0.90 + 0.80 + 0.10) = 2.75/Z$$

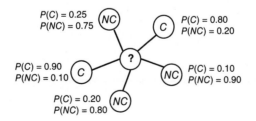

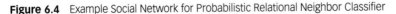

Figure 6.4 Example Social Network for Probabilistic Relational Neighbor Classifier

Since both probabilities have to sum to 1, Z equals 5, so the probabilities become:

$$P(C|?) = 2.25/5 = 0.45$$

$$P(NC|?) = 2.75/5 = 0.55$$

RELATIONAL LOGISTIC REGRESSION

Relational logistic regression was introduced by Lu and Getoor.[4] It basically starts off from a data set with local node-specific characteristics and adds network characteristics to it, as follows:

- Most frequently occurring class of neighbor (mode-link)
- Frequency of the classes of the neighbors (count-link)
- Binary indicators indicating class presence (binary-link)

This is illustrated in Figure 6.5.

A logistic regression model is then estimated using the data set with both local and network characteristics. Note that there is some correlation between the network characteristics added, which should be filtered out during an input selection procedure (e.g., using stepwise logistic regression). This idea is also referred to as featurization, since the network characteristics are basically added as special

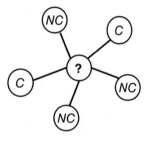

CID	Age	Income	...	Mode link	Frequency no churn	Frequency churn	Binary no churn	Binary churn
Bart	33	1,000		NC	3	2	1	1

Figure 6.5 Relational Logistic Regression

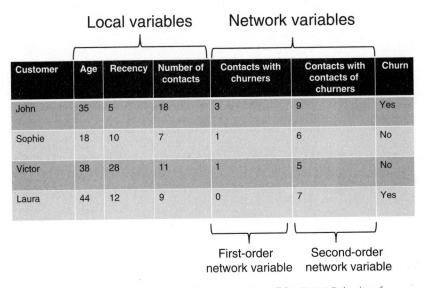

Customer	Age	Recency	Number of contacts	Contacts with churners	Contacts with contacts of churners	Churn
John	35	5	18	3	9	Yes
Sophie	18	10	7	1	6	No
Victor	38	28	11	1	5	No
Laura	44	12	9	0	7	Yes

Figure 6.6 Example of Featurization with Features Describing Target Behavior of Neighbors

features to the data set. These features can measure the behavior of the neighbors in terms of the target variable (e.g., churn or not) or in terms of the local node-specific characteristics (e.g., age, promotions, RFM). Figure 6.6 provides an example, whereby features are added describing the target behavior (i.e., churn) of the neighbors. Figure 6.7 provides an example, whereby features are added describing the local node behavior of the neighbors.

Customer	Age	Average duration	Average revenue	Promotions	Average age friends	Average duration friends	Average revenue friends	Promotions friends	Churn
John	25	50	123	X	20	55	250	X	Yes
Sophie	35	65	55	Y	18	44	66	Y	No
Victor	50	12	85	None	50	33	50	X, Y	No
Laura	18	66	230	X	65	55	189	X	No

Figure 6.7 Example of Featurization with Features Describing Local Node Behavior of Neighbors

COLLECTIVE INFERENCING

Given a network initialized by a local model and a relational model, a collective inference procedure infers a set of class labels/probabilities for the unknown nodes by taking into account the fact that inferences about nodes can mutually affect one another. Some popular examples of collective inferencing procedures are:

- Gibbs sampling[5]
- Iterative classification[6]
- Relaxation labeling[7]
- Loopy belief propagation[8]

As an example, Gibbs sampling works as follows:

1. Given a network with known and unknown nodes, initialize every unknown node using the local classifier to obtain the (local) posterior probabilities $P(c = k)$, $k = 1, ..., m$ (m = number of classes).

2. Sample the class value of each node according to the probabilities $P(c = k)$.

3. Generate a random ordering for the unknown nodes.

4. For each node i in the ordering
   a. Apply the relational learner to node i to obtain new posterior probabilities $P(c = k)$.
   b. Sample the class value of each node according to the new probabilities $P(c = k)$.

5. Repeat step 5 during 200 iterations without keeping any statistics (burning period).

6. Repeat step 5 during 2,000 iterations counting the number of times each class is assigned to a particular node. Normalizing these counts gives us the final class probability estimates.

Note, however, that empirical evidence has shown that collective inferencing usually does not substantially add to the performance of a social network learner.

EGONETS

While real-life networks often contain billions of nodes and millions of links, sometimes the direct neighborhood of nodes provides enough information on which to base decisions. An ego-centered network, or *egonet*, represents the one-hop neighborhood of the node of interest. In other words, an egonet consists of a particular node and its immediate neighbors. The center of the egonet is the ego, and the surrounding nodes are the alters. An example of an egonet is illustrated in Figure 6.8. Especially when networks are highly characterized by homophily, egonets can be very useful. Homophily is the tendency of people to associate with others whom they perceive as being similar to themselves in some way.[9] In such homophilic networks, the influences of the direct neighborhood are so intense that they diminish the effect of the rest of the network. Restricting the analysis to the egonet already gives a good indication of the behavior and interests of the surveyed individual: If all of John's friends have a flamboyant personality what does this say about John? The same reasoning holds in fraud networks: If all of Mary's friends are fraudsters, what kind of behavior do you expect from Mary?

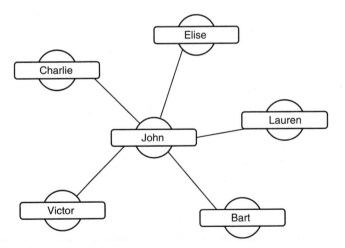

Figure 6.8 John's Egonet: The Center of the Egonet Is the Ego, the Surrounding Nodes Are the Alters of the Egonet

BIGRAPHS

Nodes in networks represent real-life objects, such as customers, patients, Internet routers, companies, and so forth. These objects are connected to each other through links. As in real-life applications, some of these relationships are stronger than others. This is reflected in the weight of the link. In call behavior data for example, two users are more closely related when they call each other more often. Authors who write various papers together have a stronger connection. Companies rely more on each other when they share more resources. All this information can be summarized in a network representation connecting nodes directly to each other and weighing the links between them. This is a *unipartite* graph, as the graph only contains one type of nodes. A unipartite graph for the author network is illustrated in Figure 6.9. The weights between nodes are represented by the thickness of the lines connecting the two nodes. Tina is more closely connected to Peter and Monique than Louis. In some applications, it can be interesting to gather more detailed information about the object that connects these nodes. In the author network, authors are explicitly connected with each other through papers. For the company network, a relationship between companies only exists when they utilize a common resource. Adding a new type of node to the network does not only enrich the imaginative power of graphs, but also creates new insights in the network structure and provides additional information

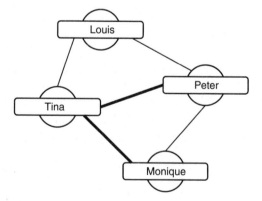

Figure 6.9 Author Network

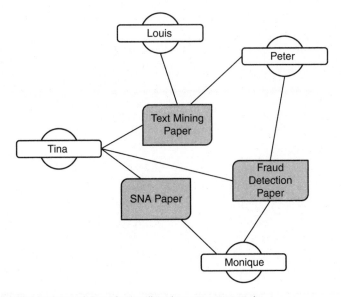

Figure 6.10 Representation of a Small Author–Paper Network

neglected before. However, including a second type of nodes results in an increasing complexity for analysis.

If a network consists of two types of nodes, we call the network a *bipartite* graph or a *bigraph*. For example, in an author–paper network, there are two types of nodes: authors and papers. This is illustrated in Figure 6.10. Mathematically, a bipartite graph is represented by a matrix M with n rows and m columns. The rows refer to the type-one nodes, while the columns specify the type-two nodes. The corresponding matrix of Figure 6.10 is given in Figure 6.11.

		Paper		
		TM	SNA	FD
Author	Louis	1	–	–
	Tina	1	1	1
	Peter	1	–	1
	Monique	–	1	1

Figure 6.11 Mathematical Representation of the Author–Paper Network

While the weight of the links in the unipartite graph was used to represent the frequency that both nodes were associated to a similar object (e.g., the number of papers written together), the bipartite graph allows one to include additional information in the link weight, like the recency, intensity, and information exchange. For example, in the author–paper network, instead of using a binary link (0/1 or writer/ nonwriter) to specify relationships between authors and papers, the link weight can now represent the contributions of each author to the paper. When analyzing the influence of one node on another, the link weights should refer to the recency of the relationship. Authors will have much less influence on each other if they wrote a paper together several years ago than if they had written the paper only yesterday.

NOTES

1. M. Girvan and M. E. J. Newman, "Community Structure in Social and Biological Networks," in *Proceedings of the National Academy of Sciences* (2002), 7821–7826.
2. W. Verbeke, D. Martens, and B. Baesens, "Social Network Analysis for Customer Churn Prediction," *Applied Soft Computing,* forthcoming, 2014.
3. S. A. Macskassy and F. Provost, "Classification in Networked Data: A Toolkit and a Univariate Case Study," *Journal of Machine Learning Research* 8 (2007): 935–983; W. Verbeke, D. Martens, and B. Baesens, "Social Network Analysis for Customer Churn Prediction," Applied Soft Computing, forthcoming, 2014; T. Verbraken et al., "Predicting Online Channel Acceptance Using Social Network Data," *Decision Support Systems,* forthcoming, 2014.
4. Q. Lu and L. Getoor, "Link-based Classification," in *Proceedings of the Twentieth Conference on Machine Learning (ICML-2003)* (Washington, DC, 2003).
5. S. Geman and D. Geman, "Stochastic Relaxation, Gibbs Distributions, and the Bayesian Restoration of Images," *IEEE Transactions on Pattern Analysis and Machine Intelligence* 6 (1984): 721–741.
6. Q. Lu and L. Getoor, "Link-based Classification," in *Proceedings of the Twentieth Conference on Machine Learning (ICML-2003)* (Washington, DC, 2003).
7. S. Chakrabarti, B. Dom, and P. Indyk, "Enhanced Hypertext Categorization Using Hyperlinks," in *Proceedings of the 1998 ACM SIGMOD International Conference on Management of Data* (1998), ACM, Seattle, WA, US, 307–319.
8. J. Pearl, *Probabilistic Reasoning in Intelligent Systems* (Morgan Kaufmann, 1988).
9. M. E. J. Newman, *Networks: An Introduction* (Oxford University Press, 2010).

CHAPTER 7

Analytics: Putting It All to Work

I n Chapter 1, we discussed the following key requirements of analytical models:

- Business relevance
- Statistical performance
- Interpretability and justifiability
- Operational efficiency
- Economical cost
- Regulatory compliance

When only considering statistical performance as the key objective, analytical techniques such as neural networks, SVMs, and random forests are among the most powerful. However, when interpretability and justifiability are the goal, then logistic regression and decision trees should be considered. Obviously, the ideal mix of these requirements largely depends on the setting in which analytics is to be used. For example, in fraud detection, response and/or retention modeling, interpretability, and justifiability are less of an issue. Hence, it is common to see techniques such as neural networks, SVMs, and/or random forests applied in these settings. In domains such as credit risk modeling and medical diagnosis, comprehensibility is a key requirement. Techniques such as logistic regression and decision trees are very popular here. Neural networks and/or SVMs can also be applied if they are complemented with white box explanation facilities using, for example, rule extraction and/or two-stage models, as explained in Chapter 3.

BACKTESTING ANALYTICAL MODELS

Backesting is an important model monitoring activity that aims at comparing ex-ante made predictions with ex-post observed numbers.[1] For example, consider the example in Table 7.1 of a churn prediction model. The purpose here is to decide whether the observed churn rates differ significantly from the estimated probability of churn.

During model development, one typically performs out-of-sample validation. This means that the training set and test set basically stem from the same underlying time period. Backtesting is done using an out-of-sample/out-of-time data set, as illustrated in Figure 7.1. Out of universe validation refers to testing the model on another population. An example of this could be a model developed on European customers that is being validated on American customers.

Many challenges arise during backtesting. Different reasons could be behind the differences between the predicted and observed churn rates reported in Table 7.1. A first reason could be sample variation. This is the variation due to the fact that the predictions are typically based on a limited sample. Suppose one only considers sample variation and the churn rate for a cluster is 1 percent, and one wants to be 95 percent confident that the actual churn rate is no more than 20

Table 7.1 Backtesting a Churn Prediction Model

Cluster	Estimated Probability of Churn	No. of Customers Observed	No. of Churners Observed	Observed Churn Rate
A	2%	1,000	30	3%
B	4%	2,000	120	6%
C	10%	4,000	500	12.5%
D	30%	2,000	750	37.5%

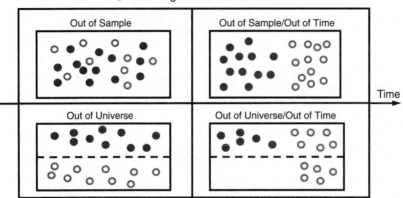

Figure 7.1 Out-of-Sample versus Out-of-Sample/Out-of-Time Validation

basis points off from that estimate. The number of observations needed would be:

$$n = \left(\frac{1.96\sqrt{P(1-P)}}{0.002} \right)^2 = 9,500$$

When dealing with large data sets, this number can be easily obtained. However, for smaller data sets (as is typically the case in credit risk modeling), a lower number of observations might be available, hereby inflating the standard errors and making the uncertainty on the predictions bigger.

External effects could also be a reason for the difference between predicted and observed churn rates. A typical example here is the impact of macroeconomic up- or downturns.

Finally, internal effects could also play a role. Examples here are a strategy change or a merger and/or acquisition. Both have an impact on the composition of the data samples and, as such, also on the observed churn rates.

When backtesting analytical models, one often adopts a traffic light indicator approach to encode the outcome of a performance metric or test statistic. A green traffic light means that the model predicts well and no changes are needed. A yellow light indicates an early warning that a potential problem may arise soon. An orange light is a more severe warning that a problem is very likely to arise. A red light then indicates a serious problem that needs immediate attention and action. Depending on the implementation, more or fewer traffic lights can be adopted.

Backtesting Classification Models

When backtesting classification models, one should first clearly state whether the goal of the classification model is scoring/ranking or providing well-calibrated posterior class probabilities. In response and/or retention modeling, one is typically interested in scores/ranking customers, whereas in credit risk modeling, well-calibrated probabilities are needed. When the model purpose is scoring, backtesting should check both data stability and model ranking. When the model is aimed at providing well-calibrated probabilities, the calibration itself should also be backtested.

When validating data stability, one should check whether internal or external environmental changes will impact the classification model. Examples of external environmental changes are new developments in economic, political, or legal environment; changes in commercial law; or new bankruptcy procedures. Examples of internal environmental changes are changes of business strategy, exploration of new market segments, or changes in organizational structure (internal). A two-step approach can be suggested as follows:

1. Check whether the population on which the model is currently being used is similar to the population that was used to develop the model.

2. If differences occur in step 1, verify the stability of the individual variables.

For step 1, a system stability index (SSI) can be calculated as follows:

$$SSI = \sum_{i=1}^{k} (observed_i - expected_i) \cdot \ln \frac{observed_i}{expected_i}$$

This is illustrated in Table 7.2.

Note that the system stability index is also referred to as the *deviation index*. It is identical to the information value measure discussed

Table 7.2 Calculating the System Stability Index (SSI)

Score Range	Expected (Training) %	Observed (Actual) %	SSI
0–169	6%	7%	0.0015
170–179	10%	8%	0.0045
180–189	9%	7%	0.0050
190–199	12%	9%	0.0086
200–209	12%	11%	0.0009
210–219	8%	11%	0.0096
220–229	7%	10%	0.0107
230–239	8%	12%	0.0162
240–249	12%	11%	0.0009
250+	16%	14%	0.0027
	100%	100%	**0.0605**

in Chapter 2 for variable screening. A rule of thumb can be defined as follows:

- SSI < 0.10: no significant shift (green traffic light)
- 0.10 ≤ SSI < 0.25: moderate shift (yellow traffic light)
- SSI ≥ 0.25: significant shift (red traffic light)

It is also recommended to monitor the SSI through time as illustrated in Table 7.3.

When population instability has been diagnosed, one can then verify the stability of the individual variables. Again, a system stability index can be calculated at the variable level as illustrated in Table 7.4. Note also that histograms and/or t-tests can be used for this purpose.

Backtesting model ranking verifies whether high (low) scores are assigned to good (bad) customers. Ranking is then typically used in combination with profit measures to decide on the desired action (e.g., who to mail in a direct mailing campaign). Performance measures commonly adopted here have been discussed in Chapter 3: ROC, CAP, lift, and/or Kolmogorov-Smirnov curves. In terms of area under the ROC curve, one can adopt the traffic light indicator approach given in Table 7.5. Note that an AUC of bigger than 0.95 can be regarded as too good to be true and might be a sign that something has gone wrong in

Table 7.3 Monitoring the SSI through Time

Score Range	Expected (Training) %	Observed (Actual) % at t	Observed (Actual) % at $t+1$
0–169	6%	7%	6%
170–179	10%	8%	7%
180–189	9%	7%	10%
190–199	12%	9%	11%
200–209	12%	11%	10%
210–219	8%	11%	9%
220–229	7%	10%	11%
230–239	8%	12%	11%
240–249	12%	11%	10%
250+	16%	14%	15%
SSI versus Expected		0.0605	0.0494
SSI versus $t-1$			0.0260

Table 7.4 Calculating the SSI for Individual Variables

	Range	Expected (Training)%	Observed (Actual)% at t	Observed (Actual) % at $t+1$
Income	0–1,000	16%	18%	10%
	1,001–2,000	23%	25%	12%
	2,001–3,000	22%	20%	20%
	3,001–4,000	19%	17%	25%
	4,001–5,000	15%	12%	20%
	5,000+	5%	8%	13%
	SSI Reference		0.029	0.208
	SSI $t-1$			0.238
Years client	Unknown client	15%	10%	5%
	0–2 years	20%	25%	15%
	2–5 years	25%	30%	40%
	5–10 years	30%	30%	20%
	10+ years	10%	5%	20%
	SSI Reference		0.075	0.304
	SSI $t-1$			0.362

Table 7.5 Traffic Light Coding of AUC

Area under the ROC Curve	Quality
$0 < AUC \le 0.5$	No discrimination
$0.5 < AUC \le 0.7$	Poor discrimination
$0.7 < AUC \le 0.8$	Acceptable discrimination
$0.8 < AUC \le 0.9$	Excellent discrimination
$0.9 < AUC \le 1$	Exceptional

the setup of the model (e.g., information about the dependent variable was used in one of the independent variables).

One can then monitor the AUC or accuracy ratio (AR) through time using a report as depicted in Table 7.6. A rule of thumb that could be applied here is that a decrease of less than 5% in terms of AR is considered green (normal script), between 5% and 10% yellow (bold face), and more than 10% red (bold face and underlined).

For backtesting probability calibration, one can first use the Brier score defined as follows:

$$\frac{1}{n}\sum_{i=1}^{n}(\hat{P}_i - \theta_i)^2$$

Table 7.6 Monitoring Accuracy Ratio (AR) through Time

	Number of Observations	Number of Defaulters	AR
AR model	5,866	105	0.85
AR 2012	5,677	97	0.81
AR 2011	5,462	108	0.80
AR 2010	5,234	111	0.83
AR 2009	5,260	123	**0.79**
AR 2008	5,365	113	**0.79**
AR 2007	5,354	120	**_0.75_**
AR 2006	5,306	119	0.82
AR 2005	4,970	98	**0.78**
AR 2004	4,501	62	0.80
AR 2003	3,983	60	0.83
Average AR	5,179.8	101.5	**0.8**

whereby n is the number of customers, $\hat{P}_i$ the calibrated probability for customer i, and θ_i is 1 if the event of interest (e.g. churn, fraud, default) took place and 0 otherwise. The Brier score always varies between 0 and 1, and lower values indicate a better calibration ability.

Another very popular test for measuring calibration performance is the binomial test. The binomial test assumes an experiment with only two outcomes (e.g., head or tail), whereby the experiment is repeated multiple times and the individual outcomes are independent. Although the last assumption is not always nicely fulfilled because of, for example, social network effects, the binomial test is often used as a heuristic for calibration. It works as follows:

H_0: The estimated probability of the event (e.g., churn, fraud, default), $\hat{P}$, equals the true probability P.

H_A: The estimated probability of the event $\hat{P}$ is bigger/smaller/not equal to the true probability.

Note that the estimated probability $\hat{P}$ is typically the probability within a particular customer segment or pool. Depending on the analytical technique, the pool can be obtained in various ways. It could be a leaf node of a decision tree, or a clustered range output from a logistic regression.

Assuming a right-tailed test and given a significance level, α, (e.g., $\alpha = 99\%$), H_0 is rejected if the number of events is greater than or equal to k^*, which is obtained as follows:

$$k^* = \min\left\{ k \mid \sum_{i=k}^{n} \binom{n}{k} \hat{P}^i (1-\hat{P})^i \leq 1-\alpha \right\}.$$

For large n, $n\hat{P} > 5$ and $n(1-\hat{P}) > 5$, the binomial distribution can be approximated by a normal distribution as $N(n\hat{P}, n\hat{P}(1-\hat{P}))$. Hence, one obtains:

$$P\left(z \leq \frac{k^* - n\hat{P}}{\sqrt{n\hat{P}(1-\hat{P})}} \right) = \alpha,$$

with z a standard normally distributed variable. The critical value, k^*, can then be obtained as follows:

$$k^* = n\hat{P} + N^{-1}(\alpha)\sqrt{n\hat{P}(1-\hat{P})}$$

with $N^{-1}(\alpha)$ the inverse cumulative standard normal distribution. In terms of a critical event rate, $p*$, one then has:

$$p* = \hat{P} + N^{-1}(\alpha)\sqrt{\frac{\hat{P}(1-\hat{P})}{n}}$$

H_0 can then be rejected at significance level α, if the observed event rate is higher than $p*$. Remember that the binomial test assumes that all observations are independent. If the observations are correlated, then the binomial test has a higher probability to erroneously reject H_0 (type I error), so that's why it is often used as an early warning system. It can be coded using traffic lights, as follows:

- Green (normal font): no statistical difference at 90 percent
- Yellow (italics): statistical difference at 90 percent but not at 95 percent
- Orange (bold face): statistical difference at 95 percent but not at 99 percent
- Red (bold face and underlined): statistical difference at 99 percent

Table 7.7 shows an example of using the binomial test for backtesting calibrated probabilities of default (PDs) against observed default rates (DRs). It can be seen that from 2001 onwards, the calibration is no longer satisfactory.

The Hosmer-Lemeshow test is a closely related test that will test calibrated versus observed event rates across multiple segments/pools simultaneously. It also assumes independence of the events, and the test statistic is defined as follows:

$$\chi^2(k) = \sum_{i=1}^{k} \frac{(n_i \hat{P}_i - \theta_i)^2}{n_i \hat{P}_i (1 - \hat{P}_i)}$$

whereby n_i is the number of observations in pool i, $\hat{P}_i$ is the estimated probability of the event for pool i, and θ_i is the number of observed events. The test statistic follows a chi-squared distribution with k degrees of freedom. It can be coded using traffic lights in a similar way as for the binomial test.

Table 7.7 The Binomial Test for Backtesting PDs versus DRs

PD	Baa1	Baa2	Baa3	Ba1	Ba2	Ba3	B1	B2	B3	Caa-C	Av
	0.26%	**0.17%**	**0.42%**	**0.53%**	**0.54%**	**1.36%**	**2.46%**	**5.76%**	**8.76%**	**20.89%**	**3.05%**
DR	Baa1	Baa2	Baa3	Ba1	Ba2	Ba3	B1	B2	B3	Caa-C	Av
1993	0.00%	0.00%	0.00%	0.83%	0.00%	0.76%	3.24%	5.04%	11.29%	28.57%	3.24%
1994	0.00%	0.00%	0.00%	0.00%	0.00%	0.59%	1.88%	3.75%	7.95%	5.13%	1.88%
1995	0.00%	0.00%	0.00%	0.00%	0.00%	1.76%	4.35%	6.42%	4.06%	11.57%	2.51%
1996	0.00%	0.00%	0.00%	0.00%	0.00%	0.00%	1.17%	0.00%	3.28%	13.99%	0.78%
1997	0.00%	0.00%	0.00%	0.00%	0.00%	0.47%	0.00%	1.54%	7.22%	14.67%	1.41%
1998	0.00%	0.31%	0.00%	0.00%	0.62%	1.12%	2.11%	7.55%	5.52%	15.09%	2.83%
1999	0.00%	0.00%	0.34%	0.47%	0.00%	2.00%	3.28%	6.91%	9.63%	20.44%	3.35%
2000	0.28%	0.00%	0.97%	0.94%	0.63%	1.04%	3.24%	4.10%	10.88%	19.65%	3.01%
2001	0.27%	0.27%	0.00%	0.51%	1.38%	2.93%	3.19%	11.07%	16.38%	34.45%	5.48%
2002	1.26%	0.72%	1.78%	1.58%	1.41%	1.58%	2.00%	6.81%	6.86%	29.45%	3.70%
Av	0.26%	0.17%	0.42%	0.53%	0.54%	1.36%	2.46%	5.76%	8.76%	20.9%	3.05%

Backtesting Regression Models

In backtesting regression models, one can also make a distinction between model ranking and model calibration. When predicting CLV, one might especially be interested in model ranking, since it is typically hard to accurately quantify CLV. However, in the majority of the cases, the aim is model calibration. For ranking, one could first consider a system stability index (SSI), as discussed before, applied to the categorized output. Also t-tests and/or histograms can be used here. For ranking, one could create a scatter plot and summarize it into a Pearson correlation coefficient (see Chapter 3). For calibration, one can calculate the R-squared, mean squared error (MSE), or mean absolute deviation (MAD) as also discussed in Chapter 3. Table 7.8 gives an example of a table that can be used to monitor the MSE.

Backtesting Clustering Models

When backtesting clustering models, one can first check the data stability by comparing the number of observations per cluster during model design with the number observed now and calculate a system stability index (SSI) across all clusters. One can also measure how the distance/proximity measures have changed on new observations by creating histograms of distances per cluster and compare the histograms of the model design data with those of new data. The

Table 7.8 Monitoring Model Calibration Using MSE

	MSE	Number of Observations	Number of Events	Traffic Light
MSE model				
MSE year t				
MSE year $t + 1$				
MSE year $t + 2$				
...				
Average MSE period 1				
Average MSE period 2				

distances can then be statistically tested using, for example, a *t*-test. One can also statistically compare the intracluster similarity with the intercluster similarity using an F-test to see whether reclustering is needed.

Developing a Backtesting Framework

In order to setup a backtesting framework, one needs to decide on the following:

- Diagnose backtesting needs
- Work out backtesting activities
- Design timetable for backtesting activities
- Specify tests and analyses to be performed
- Define actions to be taken in response to findings
- Identify why/what/who/how/when

All of the above should be described in a backtesting policy. Figure 7.2 presents an example of a digital dashboard application that could be developed for backtesting classification models. Note also that qualitative checks are included that are based on a judgment made by one or more business experts. These subjective evaluations are considered to be very important.

Once a backtesting framework has been developed, it should be complemented with an action plan. This plan will specify what to do in response to what finding of the backtesting exercise. Figure 7.3 gives an example of this. If the model calibration is okay, one can continue to use the model. If not, one needs to verify the model discrimination or ranking. If this is okay, then the solution might be to simply recalibrate the probabilities upward or downward using a scaling factor. If not, the next step is to check the data stability. If the data stability is still okay, one may consider tweaking the model. Note that this is, however, not that straightforward and will often boil down to reestimating the model (as is the case when the data stability is not okay).

Level 2: Calibration	Quantitative		Green	Yellow	Red
		Binomial	Not significant at 95% level	Significant at 95% but not at 99% level	Significant at 99% level
		Hosmer-Lemeshow	Not significant at 95% level	Significant at 95% but not at 99% level	Significant at 99% level
		Vasicek	Not significant at 95% level	Significant at 95% but not at 99% level	Significant at 99% level
		Normal	Not significant at 95% level	Significant at 95% but not at 99% level	Significant at 99% level
	Qualitative	Portfolio distribution	Minor shift	Moderate shift	Major shift
		Difference	Correct	Overestimation	Underestimation
		Portfolio stability	Minor migrations	Moderate migrations	Major migrations

Level 1: Discrimination	Quantitative		Green	Yellow	Red
		AR difference with reference model	< 5%	Between 5% and 10%	> 10%
		AUC difference with reference model	< 2.5%	Between 2.5% and 5%	> 5%
		Model significance	p-value < 0.01	p-value between 0.01 and 0.10	p-value > 0.10
	Qualitative	Preprocessing (missing values, outliers)	Considered	Partially considered	Ignored
		Coefficient signs	All as expected	Minor exceptions	Major exceptions
		Number of overrides	Minor	Moderate	Major
		Documentation	Sufficient	Minor issues	Major issues

Level 0: Data	Quantitative		Green	Yellow	Red
		SSI (current versus training sample)	SSI < 0.10	0.10< SSI< 0.25	SSI > 0.25
		SSI attribute level	SSI < 0.10	0.10< SSI< 0.25	SSI > 0.25
		t-test attribute level	p-value > 0.10	p-value between 0.10 and 0.01	p-value < 0.01
	Qualitative	Characteristic analysis	No change	Moderate change	Major change
		Attribute histogram	No shift	Moderate shift	Major shift

Figure 7.2 A Backtesting Digital Dashboard for Classification Models

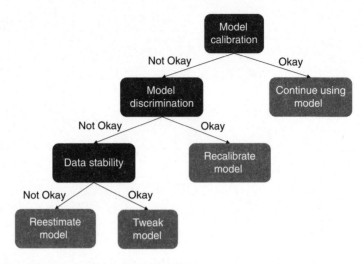

Figure 7.3 Example Backtesting Action Plan

BENCHMARKING

The idea of benchmarking is to compare the output and performance of the analytical model with a reference model or benchmark. This is needed as an extra validity check to make sure that the current analytical is the optimal one to be used. The benchmark can be externally or internally developed. A popular example of an external benchmark in credit risk modeling could be the FICO score. This is a credit score that ranges between 300 and 850 and is developed by Experian, Equifax, and Transunion in the United States. It is often used as a benchmark to compare application and/or behavioral credit scoring models. A closely related score is the Vantage score, also available in the United States. Credit rating agencies (e.g., Moody's, S&P, and Fitch) could also be considered as benchmarking partners. These agencies typically provide information on credit ratings and default probabilities that are very useful in a credit risk modeling context.

Note that although external benchmarking may seem appealing at first sight, one should be aware of potential problems, for example, unknown quality of the external benchmark, different underlying data samples and/or methodologies, different target definitions, and legal constraints. One should also be vigilant for cherry-picking, whereby the external benchmark is selected so as to correspond as closely as possible to the internal model.

The benchmark can also be internally developed, either statistically or expert based. For example, one could benchmark a logistic regression model against a neural network benchmark to see whether there are any significant nonlinearities in the data. If it turns out that this is indeed the case, then nonlinear transformations and/or interaction terms can be added to the logistic regression model to come as close as possible to the neural network performance. An expert-based benchmark is a qualitative model based on expert experience and/or common sense. An example of this could be an expert committee ranking a set of small- and medium-sized enterprises (SMEs) in terms of default risk by merely inspecting their balance sheet and financial statement information in an expert-based, subjective way.

When benchmarking, one commonly adopts a champion–challenger approach. The current analytical model serves as the champion and the benchmark as the challenger. The purpose of the challenger is to find the weaknesses of the champion and to beat it. Once the benchmark outperforms the champion, one could consider making it the new champion, and the old champion then becomes the new benchmark. The purpose of this approach is to continuously challenge the current model so as to continuously perfect it.

Popular agreement statistics for benchmarking are Spearman's rank order correlation, Kendall's τ, and the Goodman-Kruskal γ.

Spearman's rank order correlation measures the degree to which a monotonic relationship exists between the scores or ratings provided by an internal scoring system and those from a benchmark. It starts by assigning 1 to the lowest score, 2 to the second lowest score, and so on. In case of tied scores, the average is taken. Spearman's rank order correlation is then computed as follows:

$$\rho_s = 1 - \frac{6 \sum_{i=1}^{n} d_i^2}{n(n^2 - 1)}$$

whereby n is the number of observations and d_i the difference between the scores. Spearman's rank order correlation always ranges between −1 (perfect disagreement) and +1 (perfect agreement).

Kendall's τ works by first calculating the concordant and discordant pairs of observations. Two observations are said to be concordant if the observation that has a higher score assigned by the internal model also has a higher score assigned by the external model. If there is disagreement in the scores, then the pair is said to be discordant. Note that if the pair is neither concordant nor discordant, it is tied, meaning the two observations have identical scores assigned by the internal model, or by the benchmark, or by both. Kendall's τ is then calculated as follows:

$$\tau = \frac{A - B}{\frac{1}{2}n(n-1)},$$

whereby n is the number of observations, A the number of concordant pairs, and B the number of discordant pairs. Note that the denominator gives all possible pairs for n observations. Kendall's τ is 1 for perfect agreement and −1 for perfect disagreement.

Kendall's τ basically looks at all possible pairs of observations. The Goodman-Kruskal γ will only consider the untied pairs (i.e., either concordant or discordant), as follows:

$$\gamma = \frac{A - B}{A + B}$$

The Goodman-Kruskal γ is +1 if there are no discordant pairs (perfect agreement), −1 if there are no concordant pairs (perfect disagreement), and 0 if there are equal numbers of concordant and discordant pairs.

For example, consider the example in Table 7.9.

Spearman's rank order correlation then becomes −0.025. The concordant pairs are as follows: C1,C3; C1,C4; C3,C4; C3,C5; and C4,C5. The discordant pairs are: C1,C2; C2,C3; C3,C4; and C2,C5. The pair C1,C5 is a tie. Kendall's τ thus becomes: (5 − 4)/10 or 0.1 and the Goodman-Kruskal γ becomes (5 − 4)/(5 + 4) or 0.11.

In case of disagreement between the current analytical model and the benchmark, it becomes interesting to see which is the best model overall, or whether there are certain segments of observations where either the internal model or benchmark proves to be superior. Based on this analysis, it can be decided to further perfect

Table 7.9 Example for Calculating Agreement Statistics

Customer	Internal Credit Score	FICO	Rank Internal Score	Rank External Score	d_i
1	20	680	2.5	3	0.25
2	35	580	5	1	16
3	15	640	1	2	1
4	25	720	4	5	1
5	20	700	2.5	4	2.25
				$\sum_{i=1}^{n} d_i^2$	20.5

the current analytical model or simply proceed with the benchmark as the new model.

DATA QUALITY

Corporate information systems consist of many databases linked by real-time and batch data feeds.[2] The databases are continuously updated, as are the applications performing data exchange. This dynamism has a negative impact on data quality (DQ), which is very disadvantageous since DQ determines the value of the data to the analytical technique. Information and communication technology can be used to further improve intrinsic value. Hence, high-quality data in combination with good technology gives added value, whereas poor-quality data with good technology is a big problem (remember the garbage in, garbage out idea discussed in Chapter 2). Decisions made based on bad data can create high losses for companies. Poor DQ impacts organizations in many ways. At the operational level, it has an impact on customer satisfaction, increases operational expenses, and will lead to lowered employee job satisfaction. Similarly, at the strategic level, it affects the quality of the (analytical) decision making process.[3]

Poor DQ are often experienced in everyday life. For example, the mistaken delivery of a letter is often associated with malfunctioning postal services. However, one of the causes of this mistaken delivery can be an error in the address. Similarly, two similar emails sent to the same recipient can be an indication of a duplication error.

Moreover, the magnitude of DQ problems is continuously growing following the exponential increase in the size of databases. This certainly qualifies DQ management as one of the most important business challenges in today's information-based economy.

Data quality is often defined as "fitness for use," which implies the relative nature of the concept.[4] Data with quality for one use may not be appropriate for another use. For instance, the extent to which data is required to be complete for accounting tasks may not be required for analytical sales prediction tasks. More generally, data that are of acceptable quality in one decision context may be perceived to be of poor quality in another decision context, even by the same individual. This is mainly because DQ is a multidimensional concept in which each dimension represents a single aspect or construct of data items and also comprises both objective and subjective aspects. Some aspects are independent while others depend on the type of task and/or experience of the data user. Therefore, it is useful to define DQ in terms of its dimensions. Table 7.10 shows the different DQ dimensions, their categories, and definitions.[5]

Accuracy indicates whether the data stored are the correct values. For example if my birthdate is February 27, 1975, for a database that expects dates in USA format, 02/27/1975 is the correct value. However, for a database that expects a European representation, the date 02/27/1975 is incorrect; instead 27/02/1975 is the correct value.[6]

Another interesting dimension concerns the completeness of data. The completeness dimension can be considered from different perspectives. Schema completeness refers to the extent to which entities and attributes are not lacking from the schema. Column completeness verifies whether a column of a table has missing values or not. Finally, population completeness refers to the degree to which members of the population are not present. As an example, population completeness is depicted in Table 7.11.[7]

Table 7.10 Data Quality Dimensions

Category	Dimension	Definition: The Extent to Which . . .
Intrinsic	Accuracy	Data are regarded as correct
	Believability	Data are accepted or regarded as true, real, and credible
	Objectivity	Data are unbiased and impartial
	Reputation	Data are trusted or highly regarded in terms of their source and content
Contextual	Value-added	Data are beneficial and provide advantages for their use
	Completeness	Data values are present
	Relevancy	Data are applicable and useful for the task at hand
	Appropriate amount of data	The quantity or volume of available data is appropriate
Representational	Interpretability	Data are in appropriate language and unit and the data definitions are clear
	Ease of understanding	Data are clear without ambiguity and easily comprehended
Accessibility	Accessibility	Data are available or easily and quickly retrieved
	Security	Access to data can be restricted and hence kept secure

Table 7.11 Population Completeness

ID	Name	Surname	Birth Date	Email
1	Monica	Smith	04/10/1978	smith@abc.it
2	Yuki	Tusnoda	04/03/1968	Null[a]
3	Rose	David	02/01/1937	Null[b]
4	John	Edward	14/12/1955	Null[c]

[a]Not existing
[b]Existing but unknown
[c]Not known if existing

Tuple 2: Since the person represented by tuple 2 has no email address, we can say that the tuple is complete.

Tuple 3: Since the person represented by tuple 3 has an email, but its value is not known, we can say that the tuple is incomplete.

Tuple 4: If we do not know the person represented by tuple 4 has an email or not, incompleteness may not be the case.

A next data quality dimension is believability, which is the extent to which data is regarded as true and credible.

Accessibility refers to how easy the data can be located and retrieved. From a decision making viewpoint, it is important that the data can be accessed and delivered on time, so as to not needlessly delay important decisions.

The dimension of consistency can be considered from various perspectives. A first example is the presence of redundant data (e.g. name, address, ...) in multiple data sources.

Another perspective is the consistency between related data attributes. For example, city name and zip code should be corresponding. Another consistency perspective concerns the data format used. For example, gender can be encoded as male/female, M/F, or 0/1. It is of key importance that a uniform coding scheme is adopted so as to have a consistent corporate wide data representation.

The timeliness dimension reflects how up-to-date the data is with respect to the task for which it is used.

There are different DQ problem causes such as:

- Multiple data sources: Multiple sources of the same data may produce duplicates; a consistency problem.
- Subjective judgment: Subjective judgment can create data bias; objectivity problem.
- Limited computing facilities: Lack of sufficient computing facilities limits data access; accessibility problem.
- Size of data: Big data can give high response times; accessibility problem.

Data quality can be improved through a total data quality management program. It consists of the four phases, as shown in Figure 7.4.[8]

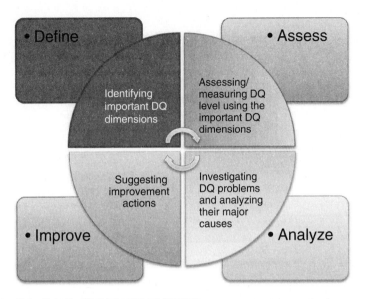

Figure 7.4 Data Quality Management Program

SOFTWARE

Different types of software can be used for doing analytics. A first distinction can be made between open source and commercial software. Popular open source analytical workbenches are RapidMiner (formerly Yale), R, and Weka. Especially the latter has gained in importance and usage nowadays. In the commercial area, SAS, SPSS, Matlab, and Microsoft are well-known vendors of analytical software. Many of these vendors actually provide analytical solutions targeted at specific industries (e.g., churn prediction in telco, fraud detection in insurance) and hereby provide full coverage of the whole range of analytical activities needed in the specific business setting.

Table 7.12 presents an overview of a KDnuggets poll asking about software used in 2012 and 2013.

Based on Table 7.12, it can be concluded that RapidMiner and R, two open source software solutions, are the most popular tools for analytics. The distinction between open source and commercial is getting more and more difficult to make, since vendors like RapidMiner have also started providing commercial versions of their software.

Table 7.12 Results of KDnuggets Poll on Software Tools Used in Analytics in 2012 and 2013.

Legend: Bold: Free/Open Source tools Normal case: Commercial tools	First bar: % users in 2013 Second bar: % users in 2012
Rapid-I RapidMiner/RapidAnalytics free edition (737), 30.9% alone	39.2% 26.7%
R (704), 6.5% alone	37.4% 30.7%
Excel (527), 0.9% alone	28.0% 29.8%
Weka/Pentaho (269), 5.6% alone	14.3% 14.8%
Python with any of numpy/scipy/ pandas/iPython packages (250), 0% alone	13.3% 14.9%
Rapid-I RapidAnalytics/RapidMiner Commercial Edition (225), 52.4% alone	12.0%
SAS (202), 2.0% alone	10.7% 12.7%
MATLAB (186), 1.6% alone	9.9% 10.0%
StatSoft Statistica (170), 45.9% alone	9.0% 14.0%
IBM SPSS Statistics (164), 1.8% alone	8.7% 7.8%
Microsoft SQL Server (131), 1.5% alone	7.0% 5.0%
Tableau (118), 0% alone	6.3% 4.4%
IBM SPSS Modeler (114), 6.1% alone	6.1% 6.8%
KNIME free edition (110), 1.8% alone	5.9% 21.8%
SAS Enterprise Miner (110), 0% alone	5.9% 5.8%
Rattle (84), 0% alone	4.5%
JMP (77), 7.8% alone	4.1% 4.0%
Orange (67), 13.4% alone	3.6% 5.3%
Other free analytics/data mining software (64), 3.1% alone	3.4% 4.9%
Gnu Octave (54), 0% alone	2.9%

Source: www.kdnuggets.com/polls/2013/analytics-big-data-mining-data-science-software.html.

In addition, Microsoft Excel is still quite popular for doing analytics. The average number of tools used was 3.

PRIVACY

The introduction of new technology, such as data analytics, brings new privacy concerns. Privacy issues can arise in two ways.[9] First, data about individuals can be collected without these individuals being aware of it. Second, people may be aware that data is collected about them, but have no say in how the data is being used. Furthermore, it is important to note that data analytics brings extra concerns regarding privacy as compared to simple data collection and data retrieval from databases.

Data analytics entails the use of massive amounts of data—possibly combined from several sources, including the Internet—to mine for hidden patterns. Hence, this technology allows for the discovery of previously unknown relationships without the customer and company being able to anticipate this knowledge. Consider an example in which three independent pieces of information about a certain customer lead to the customer being classified as a long-term credit risk, whereas the individual pieces of information would never have led to this conclusion. It is exactly this kind of discovery of hidden patterns that forms an additional threat to citizens' privacy.

Moreover, previous work has shown that it is possible to construct partial profiles of a person by crawling the web for small amounts of nonsensitive information that is publicly available; often this information is voluntarily published by individuals through social networking sites.[10] Also, the individual pieces of nonsensitive information are not harmful for one's privacy. However, when all information is aggregated into a partial profile, this information can be used for criminal activities—such as stalking, kidnapping, identity theft, phishing, scams—or for direct marketing by legitimate companies. It is again important to note that this use of data is not anticipated by citizens, hence privacy issues arise.

As illustrated by the previous examples, data analytics is more than just data collection and information retrieval from vast databases. This is recognized by the definition of data mining in several government reports. For example, the U.S. Government Accountability Office[11] defined data mining as:

> the application of database technology and techniques—such as statistical analysis and modeling—to uncover hidden patterns and subtle relationships in data and to infer rules that allow for the prediction of future results.

In the August 2006 Survey of DHS Data Mining Activities, the Department of Homeland Security (DHS) Office of the Inspector General (OIG) defined data mining as:[12]

> the process of knowledge discovery, predictive modeling, and analytics. Traditionally, this involves the discovery of patterns and relationships from structured databases of historical occurrences.

Several other definitions have been given, and generally these definitions imply the discovery of hidden patterns and the possibility for predictions. Thus, simply summarizing historical data is not considered data mining.

There are several regulations in place in order to protect an individual's privacy. The Fair Information Practice Principles (FIPPs), which were stated in a report of the U.S Department of Health, Education and Welfare in 1973,[13] have served as the main inspiration for the Privacy Act of 1974. In 1980, the Organization for Economic Cooperation and Development (OECD) defined its "Guidelines on the Protection of Privacy and Transborder Flows of Personal Data." The following basic principles are defined to safeguard privacy:[14]

- Collection limitation principle: Data collection should be done lawfully and with knowledge and consent of the data subject.
- Data quality principle: The data should be relevant for the purpose it is collected for, accurate, complete, and up-to-date.
- Purpose specification principle: The purposes of the data should be specified before data collection and the use should be limited to these purposes.
- Use limitation principle: The data should not be used for other purposes than specified, neither should it be disclosed to other

parties without consent of the data subject (or by the authority of law).

- Safety safeguards principle: The data should be protected against risks of loss, unauthorized access, use, modification, or disclosure of data.

- Openness principle: There should be a policy of openness about the developments, practices, and policies with respect to personal data.

- Individual participation principle: An individual has the right to obtain confirmation whether data exists about him or her, to receive the data, to challenge data relating to him or her and to have it erased or completed should the challenge be successful.

- Accountability principle: A data controller can be held accountable for compliance with the above principles.

These guidelines are widely accepted, have been endorsed by the U.S. Department of Commerce, and are the foundation of privacy laws in many other countries (e.g., Australia, Belgium).

Given the increasing importance and awareness of privacy in the context of analytics, more and more research is being conducted on privacy preserving data mining algorithms. The parties that are typically involved are: the record owner, the data publisher, and the data recipient.[15] A data publisher can be untrusted, in which case the collection of records needs to be done anonymously. When the data publisher is trusted, the record owners are willing to share their information with the data publisher, but not necessarily with third parties, and it is necessary to anonymize the data. This can be further complicated when the data publisher is a nonexpert in the sense that he or she is not aware that (and how) the data recipient can mine the data.

The privacy of an individual is breached when an attacker can learn anything extra about a record owner, possibly with the presence of any background knowledge from other sources.[16] Consider an example in which explicit identifiers are removed from a data set, but there is a combination of a number of variables (e.g., age, zip code, gender), which serves as a quasi-identifier (QID). This means that it is possible to link the record owner, by means of the QID, to a record

Zip Code	Age	Gender
83661	26	M
83659	23	M
83645	58	F

➡

Zip Code	Age	Gender
836**	2*	M
836**	2*	M
836**	5*	F

Figure 7.5 Example of Generalization and Suppression to Anonymize Data

owner in another data set. To preserve privacy, there should be several records in the data set with the same QID.

There are several classes of methods to anonymize data.[17] A first class of methods is generalization and suppression. These methods will remove information from the quasi-identifiers, until the records are not individually identifiable, as illustrated in Figure 7.5.

Another group of techniques consists of anatomization and permutation, which groups and shuffles sensitive values within a QID group, in order to remove the relationship between the QID and sensitive attributes. Perturbation methods change the data by adding noise, swapping values, creating synthetic data, and so forth, based on the statistical properties of the real data.[18]

MODEL DESIGN AND DOCUMENTATION

Some example questions that need to be answered from a model design perspective are:

- When was the model designed, and by who?
- What is the perimeter of the model (e.g., counterparty types, geographical region, industry sectors)?
- What are the strengths and weaknesses of the model?
- What data were used to build the model? How was the sample constructed? What is the time horizon of the sample?
- Is human judgment used, and how?

It is important that all of this is appropriately documented. In fact, all steps of the model development and monitoring process should be adequately documented. The documentation should be transparent and comprehensive. It is advised to use document management systems with appropriate versioning facilities to keep track of the different versions of the documents. An ambitious goal here is to aim for a documentation test, which verifies whether a newly hired analytical team could use the existing documentation to continue development or production of the existing analytical model(s).

CORPORATE GOVERNANCE

From a corporate governance perspective, it is also important that the ownership of the analytical models is clearly claimed. A good practice here is to develop model boards that take full responsibility of one or more analytical models in terms of their functioning, interpretation, and follow-up. Also, it is of key importance that the board of directors and senior management are involved in the implementation and monitoring processes of the analytical models developed. Of course, one cannot expect them to know all underlying technical details, but they should be responsible for sound governance of the analytical models. Without appropriate management support, analytical models are doomed to fail. Hence, the board and senior management should have a general understanding of the analytical models. They should demonstrate active involvement on an ongoing basis, assign clear responsibilities, and put into place organizational procedures and policies that will allow the proper and sound implementation and monitoring of the analytical models. The outcome of the monitoring and backtesting exercise must be communicated to senior management and, if needed, accompanied by appropriate (strategic) response. Given the strategic importance of analytical models nowadays, one sees a strong need to add a Chief Analytics Officer (CAO) to the board of directors to oversee analytic model development, implementation, and monitoring.

NOTES

1. E. Lima, C. Mues, and B. Baesens, "Monitoring and Backtesting Churn Models," *Expert Systems with Applications* 38, no. 1 (2010): 975–982; G. Castermans et al., "An Overview and Framework for PD Backtesting and Benchmarking." Special issue, *Journal of the Operational Research Society* 61 (2010): 359–373.

2. H. T. Moges et al., "A Multidimensional Analysis of Data Quality for Credit Risk Management: New Insights and Challenges," *Information and Management,* 50:1, 43–58, 2014.

3. A. Maydanchik, *Data Quality Assessment* (Bradley Beach, NJ: Technics Publications, 2007), 20–21.

4. R. Y. Wang and D. M. Strong, "Beyond Accuracy: What Data Quality Means to Data Consumers," *Journal of Management Information Systems* 12, no. 4 (1996): 5–33.

5. Ibid.

6. Y. W. Lee, L. L. Pipino, J. D. Funk, and R. Y. Wang, *Journey to Data Quality* (London: MIT Press, 2006), 67–108.

7. C. Batini and M. Scannapieco, *Data Quality: Concepts, Methodologies and Techniques* (New York: Springer, 2006), 20–50.

8. G. Shankaranarayanan, M. Ziad, and R. Y. Wang, "Managing Data Quality in Dynamic Decision Environments: An Information Product Approach," *Journal of Database Management* 14, no. 4 (2003): 14–32.

9. H. T. Tavani, "Informational Privacy, Data Mining, and the Internet," *Ethics and Information Technology* 1, no. 2 (1999): 137–145.

10. M. Pontual et al., "The Privacy in the Time of the Internet: Secrecy vs Transparency," in *Proceedings of the Second ACM Conference on Data and Application Security and Privacy* (ACM, 2012), ACM, New York, US, 133–140.

11. U.S. General Accounting Office (GAO), "Data Mining: Federal Efforts Cover a Wide Range of Uses," GAO-04-548 (May 2004), www.gao.gov/new.items/d04548.pdf.

12. U.S. Department of Homeland Security, Survey of DHS Data Mining Activities, August 2006.

13. The report is entitled "Records, Computers and the Rights of Citizens."

14. The documentation can be found at www.oecd.org/internet/ieconomy/oecdguideli nesontheprotectionofprivacyandtransborderflowsofpersonaldata.htm.

15. B. Fung et al., "Privacy-Preserving Data Publishing: A Survey of Recent Developments," *ACM Computing Surveys (CSUR)* 42, no. 4 (2010): 14.

16. T. Dalenius, "Finding a Needle in a Haystack—or Identifying Anonymous Census Record, *Journal of Official Statistics* 2, no. 3 (1986): 329–336.

17. B. Fung et al., "Privacy-Preserving Data Publishing: A Survey of Recent Developments," *ACM Computing Surveys (CSUR)* 42, no. 4 (2010): 14.

18. For more details about the specific techniques, the reader is referred to overview papers such as J. Wang et al., "A Survey on Privacy Preserving Data Mining," in *First International Workshop on Database Technology and Applications* (IEEE, Washington, DC, US, 2009), 111–114; and B. Fung et al., "Privacy-Preserving Data Publishing: A Survey of Recent Developments," *ACM Computing Surveys (CSUR)* 42, no. 4 (2010): 14.

CHAPTER 8

Example
Applications

A nalytics is hot and is being applied in a wide variety of settings. Without claiming to be exhaustive, in this chapter, we will briefly zoom into some key application areas. Some of them have been around for quite some time, whereas others are more recent.

CREDIT RISK MODELING

The introduction of compliance guidelines such as Basel II/Basel III has reinforced the interest in credit scorecards. Different types of analytical models will be built in a credit risk setting.[1] A first example are application scorecards. These are models that score credit applications based on their creditworthiness. They are typically constructed by taking two snapshots of information: application and credit bureau information at loan origination and default status information 12 or 18 months ahead. This is illustrated in Figure 8.1.

Table 8.1 provides an example of an application scorecard.

Logistic regression is a very popular application scorecard construction technique due to its simplicity and good performance.[2] For the scorecard in Table 8.1, the following logistic regression with WOE coding was used:

$$P(Customer = good \mid age, employment, salary)$$

$$= \frac{1}{1 + e^{-\left(\beta_0 + \beta_1 WOE_{age} + \beta_2 WOE_{employment} + \beta_3 WOE_{salary}\right)}}$$

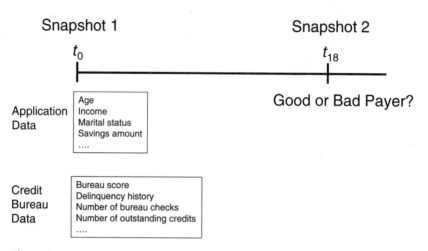

Figure 8.1 Constructing a Data Set for Application Scoring

Typically, the model will then be re-expressed in terms of the log odds, as follows:

$$\log\left(\frac{P(Customer = good|age, employment, salary)}{P(Customer = bad|age, employment, salary)}\right)$$
$$= \beta_0 + \beta_1 WOE_{age} + \beta_2 WOE_{employment} + \beta_3 WOE_{salary}$$

One then commonly applies a scorecard scaling by calculating a score as a linear function of the log odds, as follows:

$$Score = offset + factor * \log(odds)$$

Table 8.1 Example Application Scorecard

Characteristic Name	Attribute	Points
Age 1	Up to 26	100
Age 2	26–35	120
Age 3	35–37	185
Age 4	37+	225
Employment status 1	Employed	90
Employment status 2	Unemployed	180
Salary 1	Up to 500	120
Salary 2	501–1,000	140
Salary 3	1,001–1,500	160
Salary 4	1,501–2,000	200
Salary 5	2,001+	240

Assume that we want a score of 600 for odds of 50:1, and a score of 620 for odds of 100:1. This gives the following:

$$600 = \text{offset} + \text{factor} * \log(50)$$

$$620 = \text{offset} + \text{factor} * \log(100)$$

The offset and factor then become:

$$\text{factor} = 20/\ln(2)$$

$$\text{offset} = 600 - \text{factor} * \ln(50)$$

Once these values are known, the score becomes:

$$\text{Score} = \left(\sum_{i=1}^{N} (WOE_i * \beta_i) + \beta_0 \right) * \text{factor} + \text{offset}$$

$$\text{Score} = \left(\sum_{i=1}^{N} \left(WOE_i * \beta_i + \frac{\beta_0}{N} \right) \right) * \text{factor} + \text{offset}$$

$$\text{Score} = \left(\sum_{i=1}^{N} \left(WOE_i * \beta_i + \frac{\beta_0}{N} \right) * \text{factor} + \frac{\text{offset}}{N} \right)$$

Hence, the points for each attribute are calculated by multiplying the weight of evidence of the attribute with the regression coefficient of the characteristic, then adding a fraction of the regression intercept, multiplying the result by the factor, and finally adding a fraction of the offset.

In addition to application scorecards, behavioral scorecards are also typically constructed. These are analytical models that are used to score the default behavior of an existing portfolio of customers. On top of the application characteristics, behavioral characteristics, such as trends in account balance or bureau score, delinquency history, credit limit increase/decrease, and address changes, can also be used. Because behavioral scorecards have more data available than application scorecards, their performance (e.g., measured using AUC) will be higher. Next to debt provisioning, behavioral scorecards can also be used for marketing (e.g., up/down/cross-selling) and/or proactive debt collection. Figure 8.2 gives an example of how a data set for behavioral scoring is typically constructed.

Both application and behavioral scorecards are then used to calculate the probability of default (PD) for a portfolio of customers. This

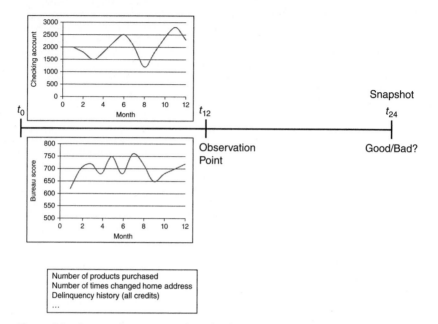

Figure 8.2 Constructing a Data Set for Behavioral Scoring

is done by first segmenting the scores into risk ratings and then calculating a historically observed default rate for each rating, which is then used to project the probability of default (PD) for (typically) the upcoming year. Figure 8.3 gives an example of how credit risk models are commonly applied in many bank settings.[3]

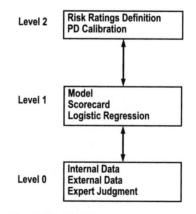

Figure 8.3 Three Level Credit Risk Model

Other measures that need to be calculated in credit risk modeling are the loss given default (LGD) and exposure at default (EAD). LGD measures the economic loss expressed as a percentage of the outstanding loan amount and is typically estimated using linear regression or regression trees. EAD represents the outstanding balance for on-balance sheet items (e.g., mortgages, installment loans). For off-balance sheet items (e.g., credit cards, credit lines), the EAD is typically calculated as follows: EAD = DRAWN + CCF * (LIMIT–DRAWN), whereby DRAWN represents the already drawn balance, LIMIT the credit limit, and CCF the credit conversion factor, which is expressed as a percentage between 0 and 1. CCF is typically modeled using either averages, linear regression, or regression trees.

Once the PD, LGD, and EAD have been estimated, they will be input into a capital requirements formula provided in the Basel II/III accord, calculating the necessary amount of capital needed to protect against unexpected losses.

FRAUD DETECTION

Fraud detection comes in many flavors. Typical examples for which fraud detection is relevant are: credit card fraud, insurance claim fraud, money laundering, tax evasion, product warranty fraud, and click fraud. A first important challenge in fraud detection concerns the labeling of the transactions as fraudulent or not. A high suspicion does not mean absolute certainty, although this is often used to do the labeling. Alternatively, if available, one may also rely on court judgments to make the decision.

Supervised, unsupervised, and social network learning can be used for fraud detection. In supervised learning, a labeled data set with fraud transactions is available. A common problem here is the skewness of the data set because typically only a few transactions will be fraudulent. Hence, a decision tree already starts from a very pure root node (say, 99 percent nonfraudulent/1 percent fraudulent) and one may not be able to find any meaningful splits to further reduce the impurity. Similarly, other analytical techniques may have a tendency to simply predict the majority class by labeling each transaction as nonfraudulent. Common schemes to deal with this are over- and undersampling. In oversampling, the fraudulent transactions in the training data set (not the test data set!) are replicated to increase their importance. In undersampling, nonfraudulent transactions are removed from the training data set (not test data set!) to increase the weight and importance of the fraudulent transactions. Both procedures are useful to help the analytical technique in finding a discriminating pattern between fraudulent and nonfraudulent transactions. Note that it is important to remember that the test set remains untouched during this. However, if an analytical technique is built using under- or oversampling, the predictions it produces on the test data set may be biased and need to be adjusted. One way to adjust the predictions is as follows:[4]

$$p(C_i|x) = \frac{\dfrac{p(C_i)}{p_t(C_i)} p_t(C_i|x)}{\sum_{j=1}^m \dfrac{p(C_j)}{p_t(C_j)} p_t(C_j|x)}$$

whereby C_i represents the target class (e.g., C_1 is fraudulent and C_2 is nonfraudulent), $p_t(C_i|x)$ represents the probability estimated on the over- or undersampled training data set, $p_t(C_i)$ is the prior probability of class C_i on the over- or undersampled training data set, and $p(C_i)$ represents the original priors (e.g., 99/1 percent). The denominator is introduced to make sure that the probabilities sum to one for all classes.

Unsupervised learning can also be used to detect clusters of outlying transactions. The idea here is to build, for example, a SOM and look for cells containing only a few observations that might potentially indicate anomalies requiring further inspection and attention.

Finally, social network analysis might also be handy for fraud detection. Although fraud may be hard to detect based on the available variables, it is often very useful to analyze the relationships between fraudsters. Rather than a standalone phenomenon, fraud is often a carefully organized crime. Exploiting relational information provides some interesting insights in criminal patterns and activities. Figure 8.4 illustrates a fraud network. Note that this network is constructed around node 1 (in the center of the figure). Nodes in the network that are green are legitimate nodes. Red nodes are fraudulent. The network visualization gives a good impression of the difference

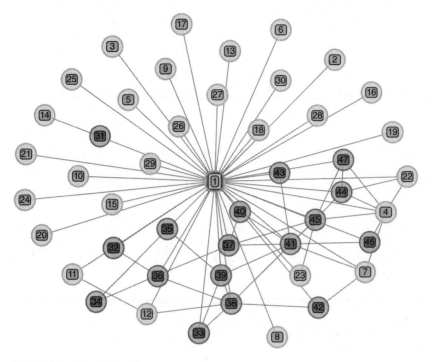

Figure 8.4 Fraud Network.
Light Gray Nodes Refer to Legitimate Individuals, While Dark Gray Nodes Represent Fraud

in network structure between legitimate and fraudulent nodes. While legitimate nodes only sparsely connect to each other, fraudulent nodes are characterized by a dense structure, with many links between all the members. Such structures have been investigated by Van Vlasselaer, Meskens, Van Dromme, and Baesens[5] and are called *spider constructions* in the domain of social security fraud. The name spider constructions is derived from their appearance: The fraudulent constructions look like a dense web in which all nodes are closely connected to each other. Based on the egonet concept, discussed earlier, both local and network variables are constructed to characterize each node. Local variables define the node of interest using only individual characteristics, independent of its surrounding neighbors. Network variables are dependent on the network structure, and include:

■ Fraudulent degree. In the network domain, the first-order degree refers to the number of immediate contacts a node has. The *n*-degree defines the number of nodes the surveyed node can reach in at most n hops. Instead of calculating the overall degree, one can make a distinction based on the label of each of the surrounding nodes. For the fraud domain, this means that the fraudulent first-order degree corresponds to counting the number of direct fraudulent neighbors.

- Triangles. A triangle in a network is defined as a structure in which three nodes of the network are connected to each other. Especially triangles containing at least two fraudulent nodes are a good indicator of potential suspicious activities of the third node. Nodes that are involved in many suspicious triangles have a higher probability to commit fraud themselves.

- Cliques. A clique is an extension of a triangle. Newman (2010) defines a clique as the maximal subset of the vertices in an undirected network such that every member of the set is connected by an edge to every other. While fraudulent triangles appear regularly in a network, fraudulent k-cliques (with $k > 3$) will appear less often. However, such cliques are extremely precise indicators of future fraud.

Although network variables as such can be very useful in detecting potential future fraud, these characteristics can also be converted in aggregated variables characterizing each node (e.g., total number of triangles/cliques, average degree weight, average triangle/clique weight). Afterward, these network variables should be enriched by local variables as discussed before. Using all the available attributes, standard learning techniques like logistic regression, random forests, and neural networks are able to estimate future fraud based on both network-related information and personal information. Such a combined approach exploits all potential information and returns the relevance, in terms of variable weight, of each characteristic.

NET LIFT RESPONSE MODELING

In response modeling, the focus lies on deepening or recovering customer relationships, or new customer acquisition by means of targeted or win-back campaigns. The campaign can be a mail catalog, email, coupon, or A/B or multivariate testing. The purpose is to identify the customers most likely to respond based on the following information:

- Demographic variables (e.g., age, gender, marital status)
- Relationship variables (e.g., length of relationship, number of products purchased)
- Social network information
- RFM variables

RFM has been popularized by Cullinan[6] as follows:

- Recency: Time frame (days, weeks, months) since last purchase
- Frequency: Number of purchases within a given time frame
- Monetary: Dollar value of purchases

Each of these constructs can be operationalized in various ways; for example, one can consider the minimum/maximum/average/most recent monetary value of purchases. The constructs can be used separately or combined into an RFM score by either independent or dependent sorting. For the former (see Figure 8.5), the customer database is sorted into independent quintiles based on RFM (e.g., recency quintile 1 is the 20 percent most ancient buyers). The final RFM score

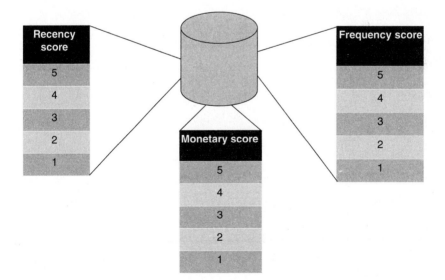

Figure 8.5 Constructing an RFM Score (Independent Sorting)

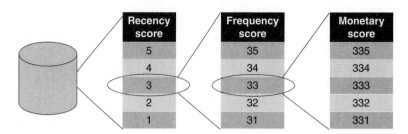

Figure 8.6　Constructing an RFM Score (Dependent Sorting)

(e.g., 325) can then be used as a predictor for the response model. For dependent sorting, the customer database is first sorted into quintiles based on recency (see Figure 8.6). Each recency quintile is then further divided into frequency quintiles and then into monetary quintiles. This again yields an RFM score (e.g., 335) that can be used as a predictor for a response model.

A first approach to response modeling is by splitting the previous campaign population into a test group and a control group (see Figure 8.7). The test group receives the marketing campaign and a model is built on a training subset and evaluated on a holdout subset. Traditionally, the impact of such a marketing campaign is measured by comparing the purchase rate of a test group against the purchase rate of a control group. If the purchase rate of the test group exceeds the purchase rate of the control group, the marketing campaign is said to be effective. Although such methods concentrate on maximizing the gross purchase rate (i.e., purchase rate test group minus purchase rate control group), they do not differentiate between different customers and therefore ignore the net or incremental impact of the campaign. In general, three types of customers can be distinguished. First, there are those people who would never buy the product, whether they are exposed to a marketing offer or not. Targeting these people would not make any sense because they won't buy the product anyway. A second group of customers is those who always buy the product. Targeting these people will cause a profit loss because they will always buy the product; therefore, offering them a marketing incentive (e.g., a discount) will reduce the profit margin. A last category of customers is the so-called swing clients. These types of customers will not buy the product spontaneously, but need to be motivated to take action.

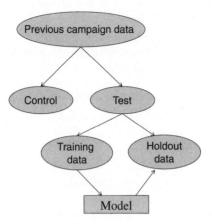

Figure 8.7 Gross Lift Response Modeling

Because they are still undecided on whether to buy the product, a marketing campaign is especially effective for these people. Focusing on only these customers will maximize the true impact of the marketing campaign and is the goal of net lift modeling. Net lift modeling tries to measure the true impact by the incremental purchases, that is, purchases that are only attributable to the campaign and that would not be made otherwise.[7] Net lift modeling aims at finding a model such that the difference between the test group purchase rate and the control group purchase rate is maximized so as to identify the swing clients (see Figure 8.8). By implementing this methodology, marketers

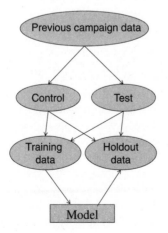

Figure 8.8 Net Lift Response Modeling

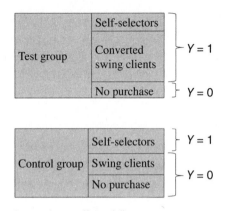

Figure 8.9 Observed Target in Net Lift Modeling

not only optimize the true business objective—maximizing profit—but also gain a better insight in the different customer segments.

In the test and control group, the target will then be observed as indicated in Figure 8.9.

One could then build a difference score model, as follows:

- Build a logistic regression model estimating probability of purchase given marketing message, $P(\text{purchase}|\text{test})$.
- Build a logistic regression model estimating probability of purchase given control, $P(\text{purchase}|\text{control})$.
- Incremental score = $P(\text{purchase}|\text{test}) - P(\text{purchase}|\text{control})$.

To further understand the impact of the predictors, one can then regress the incremental lift scores on the original data.

Another option could be to build only one logistic regression model with an additional binary predictor specifying whether an observation belongs to the control or test group. The model can then also include all possible interaction terms with this binary variable.

CHURN PREDICTION

Customer churn, also called *attrition* or *defection*, is the loss of customers. In saturated markets, there are limited opportunities to attract new customers, so retaining existing customers is essential to profitability and stability. It is estimated that attracting a new customer costs five to six times more than retaining a customer.[8] Established customers are more profitable due to the lower cost to serve them. In addition, brand loyalty developed over time makes them less likely to churn. Satisfied customers also serve as word-of-mouth advertisement, referring new customers to the company.

Research on customer churn can take two perspectives: the overall company level and the individual customer level. Identifying the determinants of churn, or reasons why customers may churn, can give insight into company-level initiatives that may reduce the issues that lead to higher churn. One such study[9] performed a survey of the Korean mobile telephone market. Service attributes such as call quality and tariff level are negatively correlated with churn in that market. Naturally, if it is possible to improve call quality, fewer customers would be expected to churn. The results of this and similar studies certainly indicate that management must focus on the quality of attributes that are most important to customers.[10] However, continually improving in these areas may not always be feasible due to cost or other limitations.

As a complementary approach, switching the focus to the individual customer level can yield high returns for a relatively low investment. It is possible to use churn prediction models to identify individual customers who are likely to churn and attempt to prevent them from leaving the company. These models assign each customer an expected probability of churn. Then it is relatively straightforward to offer those customers with the greatest probability a discount or other promotion to encourage them to extend their contract or keep their account active. In the following section, several techniques and approaches to churn prediction will be discussed.

Churn Prediction Models

Many well-known and less common models have been applied to churn prediction, including decision trees, logistic regression, support vector machines, Bayesian networks, survival analysis, self-organizing maps, and relational classifiers, among others. Both accuracy and comprehensibility are crucial for the decision-making process, so careful consideration should be used when choosing a technique. Accurate predictions are perhaps the most apparent goal, but learning the reasons, or at least the indicators, for churn is also invaluable to the company. Understanding why a model makes the predictions it does serves several purposes. Comprehensibility allows for domain experts to evaluate the model and ensure that it is intuitively correct. In this way, it can be verified or confirmed by the business. More comprehensible models also offer insight into the correlation between customer attributes and propensity to churn,[11] allowing management to address the factors leading to churn in addition to targeting the customers before they decide to churn. Finally, understandable and intuitive models may be more easily adopted within a company. If managers are accustomed to making decisions based on their own experience and knowledge, they will be more inclined to trust predictions made by a model that is not only comprehensible but also in line with their own reasoning.

Logistic regression is a statistical classification model that is often used for churn prediction, either as a model on its own or as a comparison for other models. The coefficients for this model indicate the correlation between the customer attributes and the probability of churn. It is a well understood and accepted model both in research and practice. It is both easy to interpret and provides good results when compared with other methods. It has been shown to outperform more complex methods in many cases. Decision trees can also be used for churn prediction. They also offer interpretability and robustness. Neural networks and support vector machines have also been applied to churn prediction; however, these methods are seen as black boxes, offering little insight into how the predictions are made. Survival analysis offers the interpretability of logistic regression in the form of hazard ratios that can be interpreted similarly to odds ratios in logistic regression. In addition, the target of interest is time-to-event rather than a binary variable. It is therefore possible to make predictions about how long a customer will remain active before they churn. Relational classifiers can also be used for churn prediction. Homophily in networks is based on the idea that similar individuals are more likely to interact, and from that it is expected that individuals that are connected in a network will behave similarly. In churn prediction, if customers are linked with churners, they may also be likely to churn.

Social network features can also be used in a traditional classifier like logistic regression or survival analysis. In order to do this, measures of connectedness can be extracted from the network and used as input features for the other model.[12]

Churn Prediction Process

Regardless of the particular technique, churn prediction modeling follows a standard classification process as illustrated in Figure 8.10. The first step is to define churn for the particular situation. This may be naturally present in the data: contract termination, service cancellation, or nonrenewal. In other settings, it will not be so clear: A customer no longer shops at the store or website, or a customer stops purchasing credits. In these cases, the analyst or researcher must choose a definition of churn that makes sense in the context. One common solution is to select an appropriate length of time of inactivity on the account. In the previous examples, a number of days or months without a purchase might define churn. Of course, a customer may not buy something within that time frame but still return again at a later date. Setting too short of a time period may lead to nonchurn customers being targeted as potential churners. Too long of a period may mean churning customers are not identified in a timely manner. In most cases, a shorter time period may be preferable, if the cost of the intervention campaign is much lower than the cost of a lost customer.

After defining churn, the original set of customers should be labeled according to their true churn status. The data set is split for

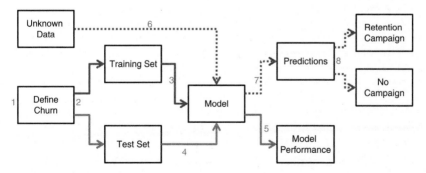

Figure 8.10 The Churn Prediction Process

validation and the customer attributes from the training set can be used to train the selected model. The customer attributes from the test set are then used to compare the model's results with the actual churn label. This allows for an evaluation of the model performance. The model may also be evaluated by domain experts to gauge whether the predictive attributes seem in line with business knowledge. If the performance is acceptable, the attributes of current customers can be entered into the model to predict their churn class. A group of customers with the highest predicted churn probability can then be contacted with the retention campaign. Other customers who are less likely to churn are not contacted with the promotion.

RECOMMENDER SYSTEMS

People are influenced by recommendations in their daily decisions. Salesmen try to sell us the product we like, restaurants are being evaluated and rated, and so on. Recommender systems can support us in our online commercial activities by suggesting specific items from a wide range of options. A considerable number of different techniques are available to build a recommender system, of which the following are the most important: collaborative filtering, content-based filtering, demographic filtering, knowledge-based filtering, and hybrid filtering. Case studies presenting all these techniques have greatly multiplied in recent years. A lot of these deal with movies,[13] tourism,[14] and restaurants.[15]

In this section, the five main techniques are introduced and followed by some of their advantages and disadvantages. Some other issues concerning recommender systems are then briefly discussed.

Collaborative Filtering

Collaborative filtering, also called *social filtering,* has been the approach that is associated the most with recommender systems. The main idea is to recommend items based on the opinions of other users. A distinction can be made between user-based collaborative filtering and item-based collaborative filtering. In case of user-based collaborative filtering, items will be recommended to a user based on how similar users rated these items. When opting for item-based collaborative filtering, items will be recommended to a user based on how this user rated similar items. One way to calculate similarity between users or items is to use a user-item matrix that contains information on which user bought what item. Any similarity measure can then be used to create a similarity matrix (e.g., Pearson correlation and cosine).

To build a collaborative recommender system, ratings are required. These ratings form the link between a user and an item.[16] A distinction can be made between three types of ratings. A scalar rating can be a number or an ordinal rating. A binary rating consists of two possibilities, such as good or bad. Finally, unary ratings indicate that a user has had an interaction with an item, such as a click on an item or a purchase.[17] We can distinguish between two types of methods for the collection of ratings. Explicit ratings can be obtained by requesting a user to rate a certain item. Implicit ratings are obtained by associating a rating with a certain action, such as buying an item.[18]

Typically, neighborhood-based algorithms are applied, in which the following three steps can be distinguished.[19] First, a similarity measure is used to calculate similarity between users (in case of a user-based algorithm) or items (in case of an item-based algorithm). Second, a subset of users or items is selected that functions as the neighborhood of the active user or item. Third, the algorithm predicts a rating based on the active user's or item's neighborhood, typically giving the highest weight to the most similar neighbors.

As is often the case with analytics, different techniques can be used to solve the same problem, with their respective advantages and disadvantages. Three main advantages of collaborative recommender systems are identified. First, collaborative filtering does not restrict the type of items to be recommended. It is indeed enough to construct a matrix linking items to users to start the recommendation. A second advantage, linked to the first, is that it manages to deliver recommendations to a user even when it is difficult to find out which specific feature of the item makes it interesting to the user or when there is no easy way to extract such a feature automatically. A third advantage has to do with novelty or serendipity: Collaborative filtering is believed to recommend more unexpected items (that are equally valuable) than content-based techniques.[20] Although collaborative filtering methods are the most commonly used techniques because of their power, some disadvantages or weak points should be noted. First, sparse data can be a problem for such a technique. A critical mass of ratings is indeed necessary in order to build meaningful similarity matrices. In cases in which the items are not frequently bought by the users (e.g., recommending mobile phones or apartments), it may indeed be difficult to obtain representative neighborhoods, hence lowering the power of the technique. A second disadvantage is known as the *cold start problem*, which means that new items cannot easily be recommended because they have not been rated yet; therefore, new users cannot easily receive recommendations because they have not yet rated items. Some minor disadvantages are, for example, the fact that items purchased a long time ago may have a substantial impact if few items have been rated, which may lead to wrong conclusions in a changing environment. Privacy could also be a problem because collaborative filtering needs data on users to give recommendations or could generate trust issues because a user cannot question the recommendation.

Content-Based Filtering

Content-based recommender systems recommend items based on two information sources: features of products and ratings given by users. Different kinds of data can be encountered, requiring different strategies to obtain usable input. In the case of structured data, each item consists of the same attributes and the possible values for these attributes are known. It is then straightforward to apply content-based approaches. When only unstructured data are available, such as text, different techniques have to be used in order to learn the user profiles. Because no standard attributes and values are available, typical problems arise, such as synonyms and polysemous words. Free text can then be translated into more structured data by using a selection of free text terms as attributes. Techniques like TF-IDF (term frequency/ inverse document frequency) can then be used to assign weights to the different terms of an item. Sometimes, data is semistructured, consisting of some attributes with restricted values and some free text. One approach to deal with this kind of data is to convert the text into structured data.[21]

When items can be represented in a usable way, machine learning techniques are applied to learn a user profile. Typically, a classification algorithm is invoked for each user based on his or her ratings on items and their attributes. This allows the recommender system to predict whether a user will like an item with a specific representation. As with collaborative filtering methods, explicit or implicit ratings are required. When explicit ratings are considered, the ratings are directly used for the classification task, whereas implicit ratings can be obtained using the item–user interactions.

The classification problem mentioned above can be implemented using a large number of different machine learning techniques. Some examples are logistic regression, neural networks, decision trees, association rules, and Bayesian networks. Nearest neighbor methods can also be used to determine the labeled items that are most similar to a new unlabeled item in order to label this new item based on the labels of the nearest neighbors. Concerning the similarity metric used in nearest neighbor methods, Euclidean distance is often used when data are structured, whereas cosine similarity may prove its use when the vector space model is applied. Other approaches are linear classifiers, support vector machines, and Naïve Bayes.[22]

A first advantage of content-based recommender systems is that there is no cold start problem for new items. Indeed, new items (which have not received ratings before) can be recommended, which was not the case in a collaborative filtering approach. Second, items can also be recommended to users that have unique preferences. A third important advantage is the possibility to give an explanation to the user about his or her recommendations, for example, by means of displaying a list of features that led to the item being recommended. A fourth advantage is that only ratings of the active user are used in order to build the profile, which is not the case for collaborative recommender systems.[23] Concerning the disadvantages, a first limitation is that content-based techniques are only suitable if the right data are available. It is indeed necessary to have enough information about the items to determine whether a user would like an item or not. The cold start problem for new users forms a second limitation as well, as old ratings potentially influence the recommendation too much. Finally, over-specialization can be a problem because such techniques will focus on items similar to the previously bought items.

Demographic Filtering

Demographic filtering recommends items based on demographic information of the user. The main challenge is to obtain the data. This can be explicitly done by asking for information from users such as age, gender, address, and so on. If this approach is not possible, analytical techniques could be used to extract information linked to the interactions of the users with the system. A user profile can then be built and used to recommend items.[24]

The main advantage of demographic recommender systems is that there is not always a need for a history of user ratings of the type that is required in collaborative and content-based approaches. Segments can be used in combination with user–item interactions in order to obtain a high-level recommender system. Some disadvantages are the cold start problem for new users and new items, as well as the difficulty in capturing the data, which is highly dependent on the participation of the users.

Knowledge-Based Filtering

Compared with collaborative filtering and content-based recommender systems, it is more difficult to briefly summarize the characteristics of knowledge-based recommender systems. The main difference with regard to the other techniques resides in the data sources used. With this approach, additional inputs consisting of constraints or requirements are provided to the recommender system typically by allowing a dialog between the user and the system. Knowledge-based recommender systems can be divided in two main categories: constraint-based recommenders and case-based recommenders. Constraint-based recommenders are systems meeting a set of constraints imposed by both users and the item domain. A model of the customer requirements, the product properties, and other constraints that limit the possible requirements is first constructed and formalized. Any technique can then be used and will have to meet the requirements, or at least minimize the violations. When dealing with case-based recommenders, the goal is to find the item that is most similar to the ones the user requires. Similarity is then often based on knowledge of the item domain. The system will then start with an example provided by the user and will generate a user profile based on it. Based on this user profile gathering information and additional knowledge sources, recommendations can then be proposed.[25]

A first advantage of knowledge-based recommender systems is that they can be used when there is only limited information about the user, hence avoiding the cold start problem. Another advantage is that expert knowledge is used in the recommender system. It is also possible to function in an environment with complex, infrequently bought items. In addition, a constraint-based recommender system can help customers actively, for example, by explaining products or suggesting changes in case no recommendation is possible. Concerning disadvantages, a knowledge-based recommender system may require some effort concerning knowledge acquisition, knowledge engineering, and development of the user interface. A second disadvantage is that it can be difficult when the user is asked to provide the system with an example if the number of items in the recommendation system is very high. Similarly, it may be difficult or impossible for the user to provide an example that fits the user's needs.

Hybrid Filtering

Hybrid recommender systems combine the advantages of content-based, knowledge-based, demographic, and collaborative filtering recommender systems. The main reason that hybrid recommender systems have been developed is to avoid the cold start problem. Burke[26] explains seven types of hybrid techniques. A first type is weighted. In this case, the recommendation scores of several recommenders are combined by applying specific weights. Switching is a second hybrid technique in which recommendations are taken from one recommender at a time, but not always the same one. A third type of hybrid technique is mixed. When such a hybrid technique is applied, recommendations for multiple recommenders are shown to the user. Feature combination is a fourth type of hybrid technique. In this case, different knowledge sources are used to obtain features, and these are then given to the recommendation algorithm. A fifth type is feature augmentation: A first recommender computes the features while the next recommender computes the remainder of the recommendation. For example, Melville, Mooney, and Nagarajan[27] use a content-based model to generate ratings for items that are unrated and then collaborative filtering uses these to make the recommendation. Cascade is the sixth type of hybrid technique. In this case, each recommender is assigned a certain priority and if high priority recommenders produce a different score, the lower priority recommenders are decisive. Finally, a meta-level hybrid recommender system consists of a first recommender that gives a model as output that is used as input by the next recommender. For example, Pazzani[28] discusses a restaurant recommender that first uses a content-based technique to build user profiles. Afterward, collaborative filtering is used to compare each user and identify neighbors. Burke[29] states that a meta-level hybrid is different from a feature augmentation hybrid because the meta-level hybrid does not use any original profile data; the original knowledge source is replaced in its entirety.

Evaluation of Recommender Systems

Two categories of evaluation metrics are generally considered:[30] the goodness or badness of the output presented by a recommender system and its time and space requirements. Recommender systems generating predictions (numerical values corresponding to users' ratings for items) should be evaluated separately from recommender systems that propose a list of N items that a user is expected to find interesting (top-N recommendation). The first category of evaluation metrics that we consider is the goodness or badness of the output presented by a recommender system. Concerning recommender systems that make predictions, prediction accuracy can be measured using statistical accuracy metrics (of which mean absolute deviation [MAD] is the most popular one) and using decision support accuracy metrics (of which area under the receiver operating characteristic curve is the most popular one). Coverage denotes for which percentage of the items the recommender system can make a prediction. Coverage might decrease in case of data sparsity in the user–item matrix. Concerning top-N recommendation, important metrics are recall precision–related measures. Data is first divided in a training set and a test set. The algorithm runs on the training set, giving a list of recommended items. The concept of "hit set"[31] is considered, containing only the recommended (top-N) items that are also in the test set. Recall and precision are then determined as follows:

$$\text{Recall} = \frac{\text{size of hit set}}{\text{size of test set}}$$

$$\text{Precision} = \frac{\text{size of hit set}}{N}$$

A problem with recall and precision is that usually recall increases as N is increased, while precision decreases as N is increased. Therefore, the $F1$ metric combines both measures:[32]

$$F1 = \frac{2 * \text{recall} * \text{precision}}{\text{recall} + \text{precision}}$$

Computing $F1$ for each user and then taking the average gives the score of the top-N recommendation list.

The other category of evaluation metrics is dealing with the performance of a recommender system in terms of time and space requirements. Response time is the time that is needed for a system to formulate a response to a user's request. Storage requirements can be considered in two ways: main memory requirement (online space needed by the system) and secondary storage requirement (offline space needed by the system).

Additional metrics can also be considered and will depend on the type of recommender system faced and the domain in which it is used. For example, it is a common practice in a direct marketing context to build a cumulative lift curve or calculate the AUC. One also has to decide whether online or offline evaluations will be made. Although offline evaluation is typically applied, it is often misleading because the context of the recommendation is not considered. However, the costs linked with online evaluations are typically higher and are accompanied by different risks (e.g., bad recommendations may impact customers' satisfaction).

Examples

Different cases applying recommendation techniques have been reported, providing the practitioners with best practices and success stories. Some references are provided in what follows, showing a small subset of the available cases. A first case that is relevant in the context of collaborative filtering is Amazon.com. Linden, Smith, and York[33] describe the use of recommendation algorithms at Amazon.com. They see recommendation systems as a type of targeted marketing because the needs of the customer can be met in a personalized way. A second case that is relevant in the context of collaborative filtering is PITTCULT, a cultural event recommender based on a network of trust. In another case, Mooney and Roy[34] apply a content-based approach on book recommendations. Semistructured text is extracted from web pages at Amazon.com and text categorization is then applied to it. Users rate books of the training set, which allows the system to learn the user profile using a Bayesian learning algorithm. A first case that is relevant in the context of knowledge-based recommender systems is "virtual advisor," the constraint-based recommender system proposed by Jannach, Zanker, and Fuchs.[35] Virtual advisor is a knowledge-based tourism recommender system that has been developed for a premium spa resort in Austria. The authors show that using a dialog, user requirements and preferences are derived. During the dialog, the internal user model is analyzed and the next dialog action is determined. When enough information is gathered about the user's requirements and preferences, the system shows the items that meet the user's constraints. If necessary, it shows which constraints have to be relaxed. A second case that is relevant in the context of knowledge-based recommender systems is Intelligent Travel Recommender (ITR), discussed by Ricci, Arslan, Mirzadeh, and Venturini.[36] ITR is a case-based travel advisory system that recommends a travel plan to a user, starting from some wishes and constraints that this user enters in the system. The current session is considered a case and it has similarities with cases of other users that are already finished. These previous cases can have an impact on the recommendation to the users. One advantage of this approach is that users do not need a login because the set of past cases that influence the user's recommendation is based on similarity between the user's case and past cases. A second advantage is that a limited user profile is sufficient, which is not the case when applying a content-based approach (as it is then assumed that users and products share features).

WEB ANALYTICS

The Digital Analytics Association (DAA) defines web analytics as:[37]

> the measurement, collection, analysis, and reporting of Internet data for the purposes of understanding and optimizing Web usage.

In what follows, we first elaborate on web data collection and then illustrate how this can be analyzed.

Web Data Collection

A key challenge in web analytics is to collect data about web visits.[38] A first option here is web server log analysis, which is essentially a server-side data collection technique making use of the web server's logging functionality. Every HTTP request produces an entry in one or more web server log files. The log file can then be parsed and processed on a set schedule to provide useful information. This is illustrated in Figure 8.11.
Common log file formats are:

- Apache/NCSA log formats: Common Log Format or Combined Log Format
- W3C (World Wide Web Consortium) Extended Log File Format and its Microsoft IIS implementation

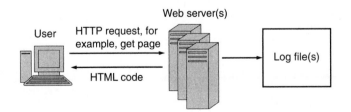

Figure 8.11 Web Server Log Analysis

```
195.162.218.155 - - [27/Jun/2011:00:01:54 +0200]
"GET /dutch/shop/detail.html HTTP/1.1" 200 38890
"http://www.msn.be/shopping/food/" "Mozilla/4.0 (MSIE 6.0)"
```

Figure 8.12 Example Log Entry

A log entry (Apache combined log format) typically looks like Figure 8.12.

The data recorded includes:

- Remote host: IP address or domain name; helps identify the geographical location of the client computer
- Remote log name ("-"); user name ("-" if no authentication)
- Date and time (can include offset from Greenwich Mean Time)
- HTTP request method (GET or POST)
- Resource requested
  - Relative to the root directory location on the web server
  - Might include query string (parameters after the ?)"GET/ dutch/shop/detail.html?ProdID=112 HTTP/1.1"
- HTTP status code
  - 200 range: successful (200 for GET request means requested resource has been sent)
  - 300 range: redirect
  - 400 range: client error (404 means not found)
  - 500 range: server error
- Number of bytes transferred
- Referrer: web page from which user clicked on link to arrive here
  - "http://www.msn.be/shopping/food/"
  - "http://www.google.com/search?q=buy+wine&hl= en&lr="
- Browser and platform (user agent)
  - Can also be a search bot, for example, Googlebot

Cookies can also be used for data collection. A cookie is a small text string that

- A web server can send to a visitor's web browser (as part of its HTTP response)
- The browser can store on the user's hard disk in the form of a small text file
- The browser sends back unchanged to that server each time a new request is sent to it (for example, when user visits another page of the site)

A cookie typically contains a unique user ID along with other customized data, domain, path (specifying from where it can be read), and expiration date (optional). Cookies can be set and read by (and their contents shared between) client-side (e.g., JavaScript) as well as server-side (e.g., PHP) scripts. A web server cannot retrieve cookies from other sites (unless by exploiting vulnerabilities, i.e., cookie stealing). Cookies are typically used for:

- Implementing virtual shopping carts
- Remembering user details or providing a customized user experience without having to log in each time
- Gathering accurate information about the site's visitors (session identification, repeat visitors)
- Banner ad tracking

A distinction can be made between session and persistent cookies. A session cookie is used to keep state info for the duration of a visit and disappears after you close the session/browser. A persistent cookie is saved to a file and kept long after the end of the session (until the specified expiration date). Another distinction relates to the originator of the cookie. A first-party cookie is set from the same domain that hosts the web page that is being visited. A third-party cookie is set by a web server from another domain, such as an ad network serving banner ads on the site that is being visited. Third-party cookies are typically used to track users across multiple sites and for behavioral targeting.

Another data collection mechanism in web analytics is page tagging. This is client-side data collection and usually involves "tagging" a web page with a code snippet referencing a separate JavaScript file that deposits and reads a cookie and sends data through to a data collection

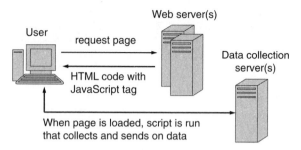

Figure 8.13 Page Tagging

server. This is illustrated in Figure 8.13. An example Google Analytics page tag is given in Figure 8.14.

With page tagging, the analytics vendor often provides a hosted service whereby the client is provided with a web interface to access reports or run analyses. A popular example of this is Google Analytics. Tables 8.2 and 8.3 illustrate the advantages and disadvantages, respectively, of page tagging versus web log analysis.

Other techniques have also been suggested for web data collection but are less commonly used, such as web beacons, packet sniffing, web server plug-ins, and/or hybrid solutions.

Web KPIs

Once the data has been collected, it can be analyzed and summarized into various web key performance indicators (KPIs). Page views are

```
<script type="text/javascript">
var gaJsHost = (("https:" == document.location.protocol) ?
"https://ssl." : "http://www.");
document.write(unescape("%3Cscript src='" + gaJsHost + "google-
analytics.com/ga.js' type='text/javascript'%3E%3C
/script%3E"));
</script>

<script type="text/javascript">
try{
var pageTracker = _gat._getTracker("UA-xxxxxx-x");    ──▶  Replace by own
pageTracker._trackPageview();                                account number
} catch(err) {}
</script>
```

Figure 8.14 Example Google Analytics Page Tag

Table 8.2 Advantages of Page Tagging versus Web Server Log Analysis

Page Tagging	Web Server Log Analysis
▪ Breaks through proxy servers and browser caching ▪ Tracks client side events (JavaScript, Flash, etc.) ▪ Easy client-side collection of outcome data (custom tags on order confirmation page) ▪ Facilitates real-time data collection and processing ▪ Often hosted service available: potential cost advantages ▪ Data capture separated from web design/programming: JavaScript code for data collection can largely be updated by in-house analysts or analytics service provider without IT department having to implement changes ▪ More innovation efforts put in by web analytics vendors	▪ Proxy/caching inaccuracies: if a page is cached, no record is logged on your web server ▪ No client-side event tracking ▪ Most often will choose to integrate with another database to obtain additional data ▪ Log files analyzed in batch (unless server plug-ins used) ▪ In-house data collection and processing ▪ Larger reliance on IT department to implement changes to capture more data ▪ Extensive preprocessing required: "stitch" together log files from different servers and filter them

the number of times a page (where *page* is an analyst-definable unit of content) was viewed. It is an important building block for other metrics, but it is not that meaningful on its own because we don't know whether the customer met his or her purpose after having visited a page. Also, in today's web environment, it might not be that straightforward to define a web page unambiguously. The next step is identifying and counting visits or sessions. An example of a visit could be: index.html ⇒ products.html ⇒ reviews.html ⇒ exit. Sessionization

Table 8.3 Disadvantages of Page Tagging versus Web Server Log Analysis

Page tagging	Web server log analysis
▪ Not including correct tags, run-time errors, and so on, mean data is lost; cannot go back ▪ Firewalls and browser privacy/security settings can hinder data collection ▪ Cannot track search engine bots/spiders/crawlers (bots do not execute tags) ▪ Less straightforward to capture technical info such as errors, bandwidth, download time, and so forth ▪ Loss of control if hosted	▪ Historical data remains available for reprocessing ▪ Server-side data collected regardless of client configuration ▪ Bots/spiders/crawlers show up in log ▪ Designed to automatically capture technical info ▪ In-house solution

is a procedure for determining which page views are part of the same visit. In defining sessions, one will make use of a combination of IP address, user agent, cookies, and/or URI parameters. Once the sessions have been defined, one could start looking at the visitors. New visitors are the unique visitors with activity including a first-ever visit to the site during a reporting period. Return visitors are the unique visitors during a reporting period who had also visited the site prior to that period. This can be interesting to determine loyalty and affinity of visitors. A next obvious question is how long/deep the visits were. This can be measured with the following metrics:

■ Page views per visit (or also visit depth, page load activity); for example, the visitor browsed through three different pages

■ Time on page

■ Time on site (also called visit duration or length); for example, the visit lasted five minutes in total

It is important to note that these metrics should be interpreted in the appropriate way. For example, a support site might want to solve the problem quickly and aim for a short time on site and/or call avoidance, whereas a content site might want to get customers engaged and aim for a longer time on site.

Another very important metric is the bounce rate. It is defined as the ratio of visits where a visitor left instantly after having seen the first page. It can be further refined as follows:

■ Bounce rate of the site: ratio of single page view visits (or bounces) over total visits

■ Bounce rate of a specific page: single page view visits of that page over number of visits where that page was the entry page

It is also important to consider the referring web page URI because it also includes search keywords and key phrases for search engine traffic sources. Other interesting measures are:

■ Most viewed pages (top content, popular pages)

■ Top entry pages

■ Top exit pages (leakage)

■ Top destinations (exit links)

Finally, a very important metric is the conversion rate. A conversion is a visitor performing an action that is specified as a useful outcome considering the purpose of the site. The conversion rate is then defined as the percentage of visits or of unique visitors for which we observed the action (e.g., order received, lead collected, newsletter sign up). It is hereby important to combine the conversion rate also with other outcome data, such as sales price, revenue, ROI, and so on.

For a checkout process, one could consider the following metrics:

- Cart abandonment rate = 1 − number of people who start checkout/total Add to Cart clicks
- Checkout abandonment rate = 1 − number of people who complete checkout/number of people who start checkout

It is important to note that small improvements in these metrics can usually lead to substantial revenue gains.

The average visits or days to purchase is a pan-session metric giving insight into how long it takes people to buy from your website (or submit a lead).

Turning Web KPIs into Actionable Insights

Ultimately, it is the purpose to transform the metrics discussed earlier into actionable insights. Each metric should be compared in time to see whether there are any significant changes. For example, popular referrers are disappearing, new referrers come in, top five referrers changed, top destinations changed, and so forth. Trend analysis is very useful here. It is important to verify whether there is an upward/downward trend, or any seasonalities or daily/weekly/monthly patterns to observe. This is illustrated in Figure 8.15 for the conversion rate.

Dashboards will be used to effectively monitor and communicate the web KPIs. They often provide intuitive indicators such as gauges, stoplights, and alerts and can be personalized.

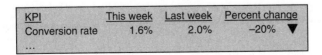

KPI	This week	Last week	Percent change
Conversion rate	1.6%	2.0%	−20% ▼
...			

Figure 8.15 Monitoring the Conversion Rate

Benchmarking can also be very useful to compare internal web KPIs against industry standards. Popular benchmark service providers are Fireclick and Google Analytics's benchmarking service.

Segmentation is also very important in order to turn web KPIs into actionable insights. Any measure can be broken down into segments of interest and aggregate (total, proportion, average) numbers can be computed per segment. For example, one could segment bounce/conversion rates by:

- Top five referrers
- Search traffic or not
- Geographical region
- Acquisition strategy (i.e., direct marketing, PPC, SEO/organic search, email marketing, newsletter, affiliates)

This can be very efficiently supported by means of OLAP facilities to perform interactive analysis of large volumes of web KPI data from multiple dimensions.

Site search reports are also very useful because they provide a basic understanding of the usage of the internal search engine. This is a basic form of market research because the users tell you exactly what they are looking for. It is interesting to consider the following:

- Site search usage
  - How much is the search function used?
  - What keywords are used most?
- Site search quality
  - Calculate bounce rate for site search (% search exits)

Navigation Analysis

Navigation analysis allows us to understand how users navigate through the website.

Path analysis gives insight into frequent navigation patterns. It analyzes, from a given page, which other pages a group of users visit next in x percent of the times. Note, however, that this assumes that the users follow a linear path, which is not always the case.

A funnel plot focuses on a predetermined sequence (e.g., a check out process) and measures entry/abandonment at each stage.

A page overlay/click density analysis shows clicks or other metrics (e.g., bounce/conversion rates) overlaid directly on actual pages such that one can traverse through the website as a group of users typically navigates through it. Heat maps then have colors indicating the click frequencies.

Again, it is important to combine all these plots with segmentation to give actionable insights.

Search Engine Marketing Analytics

Web analytics can also be used to measure the efficiency of search engine marketing. Two types of search engine marketing are search engine optimization (SEO) and pay per click (PPC). In SEO, the purpose is to improve organic search results in a search engine (e.g., Google, Yahoo!) without paying for it. This can be accomplished by carefully designing the website. In PPC, one pays a search engine for a link/ad to the website to appear in the search results. The link/ad is then listed depending on the search engine algorithm, the bid, and the competitor's bids. Popular examples are Google AdWords and Yahoo! Search Marketing. SEO efforts can be measured as follows:

- Inclusion ratio = number of pages indexed/number of pages on your website. Note that sometimes you do not want pages to be indexed, to avoid users arriving too deep within a website.
- Robot/crawl statistics report. See how frequently your website is being visited by search engine robots and how deep they get. Note that this should be done based on seb log analysis, since robots do not run JavaScript page tags.
- Track inbound links by using www.mysite.com in Google.
- Google webmaster tools that show, for the most popular search keywords or phrases that have returned pages from your site, the number of impressions or user queries for which your website appeared in the search results and the number of users who actually clicked and came to your website.

- Track rankings for your top keywords/key phrases.
- See whether keywords link to your most important pages.

PPC efforts can be tracked as follows:

- Reports that differentiate bid terms versus search terms when users enter site through PPC campaign (e.g., bid term is "laptop" but search term is "cheap laptops")
- Analyze additional data obtained about ad impressions, clicks, cost
- Keyword position report (for example, AdWords position report)
  - Specifies position your ad was in when clicked
  - Can show any metric (e.g., unique visitors, conversion rate, bounce rate) per position

A/B and Multivariate Testing

The purpose here is to set up an experiment whereby different pages or page elements are shown to randomly sampled visitors. Example pages that could be considered are landing page (first page of a visit), page in checkout process, most popular page(s), or pages with high bounce rates.

In A/B testing, one tests two alternative versions of a web page on a random sample of visitors and compares against a control group (who gets the original page). This is illustrated in Figure 8.16.

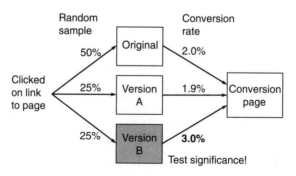

Figure 8.16 A/B Testing

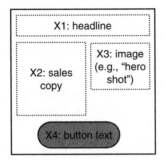

Figure 8.17 Multivariate Testing

Multivariate testing aims at testing more than one element on a page at the same time (see Figure 8.17). Note that one can also test price sensitivity or different product bundles, which requires integration with back-end data sources.

Parametric data analysis can then be used to understand the effect of individual page elements and their interactions on a target measure of interest (e.g., bounce or conversion rate). Also, techniques from experimental design can be used to intelligently decide on the various page versions to be used.

SOCIAL MEDIA ANALYTICS

With the rising popularity of the web, people are closer connected to each other than ever before. While it only has been a few years since people communicated with each other on the street, the demographic boundaries are fading away through the recently trending online communication channels. The marginal effect of traditional word-of-mouth advertising is replaced by the enormous spread of information and influence through the wires of the World Wide Web. Web users have been putting billions of data online on websites like Facebook and MySpace (social network sites), Twitter (microblog site), YouTube and DailyMotion (multimedia-sharing), Flickr and ShutterFly (photo sharing), LinkedIn and ZoomInfo (business-oriented social network site), Wikipedia and Open Directory Profound (user-generated encyclopedia), Reddit (content voting site), and many others.

Users are no longer reluctant to share personal information about themselves, their friends, their colleagues, their idols, and their political preferences with anybody who is interested in them. Nowadays, with the booming rise of mobile applications, web users are 24/7 connected to all kinds of social media platforms, giving real-time information about their whereabouts. As such, a new challenging research domain arises: social media analytics. While these data sources offer invaluable knowledge and insights in customer behavior and enable marketers to more carefully profile, track, and target their customers, crawling through such data sources is far from evident because social media data can take immense magnitudes never seen before.

From a sales-oriented point of view, social media offers advantages for both parties in the business–consumer relationship. First, people share thoughts and opinions on weblogs, microblogs, online forums, and review websites, creating a strong effect of digital word-of-mouth advertising. Web users can use others' experience to gain information and make purchase decisions. As such, consumers are no longer falling for transparent business tricks of a sales representative, but they are well-informed and make conscious choices like true experts. Public opinions are volatile. Today's zeroes are tomorrow's heroes. Companies are forced to keep offering high-quality products and services, and only a small failure can have disastrous consequences for the future. Keeping one step ahead of the competition is a tough and intensive process, especially when regional competitors are also able to enter the game. On a large scale, the main competitors for an industry used to consists of the big players of the market, while local businesses were too small and playing together with the big guys required capital-intensive investments. The Internet changed the competitive environment drastically, and consumers can easily compare product and service characteristics of both local and global competitors.

Although the merciless power of the public cannot be underestimated, companies should embrace and deploy social media data. People trust social media platforms with their personal data and interests, making it an invaluable data source for all types of stakeholders. Marketers who are searching for the most promising and profitable consumers to target are now able to capture more concrete consumer characteristics, and hence develop a better understanding of their customers. Zeng[39] described social media as an essential component of the next-generation business intelligence platform. Politicians and governmental institutions can get an impression of the public opinion through the analysis of social media. During election campaigns, studies claim that political candidates with a higher social media engagement got relatively more votes within most political parties.[40] Social media analytics is a select tool to acquire and propagate one's reputation. Also, nonprofit organizations such as those in the health sector benefit from the dissemination power of social media, anticipating, for example, disease outbreaks, identifying disease carriers, and setting up a right vaccination policy.[41]

Social media analytics is a multifaceted domain. Data available on social media platforms contain diverse information galore, and focusing on the relevant pieces of data is far from obvious and often unfeasible. While certain social media platforms allow one to crawl publicly accessible data through their API (application programming interface), most social networking sites are protective toward data sharing and offer built-in advertisement tools to set up personalized marketing campaigns. This is briefly discussed in the first subsection. The next subsections introduce some basic concepts of sentiment and network analysis.

Social Networking Sites: B2B Advertisement Tools

A new business-to-business (B2B) billion-dollar industry is launched by capturing users' information in social network websites, enabling personalized advertising and offering services for budget and impact management.

Facebook Advertising[42] is a far-evolved marketing tool with an extensive variety of facilities and services (see Figure 8.18). Depending on the goal of the advertising campaign, Facebook Advertising calculates the impact and spread of the digital word-of-mouth advertising. Facebook Advertising not only supports simple marketing campaigns such as increasing the number of clicks to a website (click rate) or page likes (like rate) and striving for more reactions on messages posted by the user (comment and share rate), but also more advanced options like mobile app engagement (download and usage rate) and website conversion (conversion rate) are provided. The conversion rate of a marketing campaign refers to the proportion of people who undertake a predefined action. This action can be an enrollment for a newsletter,

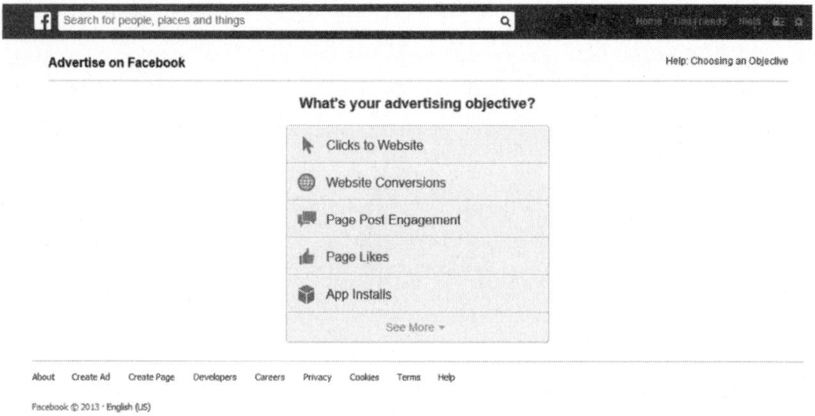

Figure 8.18   Determining Advertising Objective in Facebook Advertising

leaving an email address, buying a product, downloading a trial version, and so on, and is specific for each marketing campaign. Facebook measures conversion rates by including a conversion-tracking pixel on the web page where conversion will take place. A pixel is a small piece of code communicating with the Facebook servers and tracking which users saw a web page and performed a certain action. As such, Facebook Advertising matches the users with their Facebook profile and provides a detailed overview of customer characteristics and the campaign impact.

Facebook Advertising allows users to create personalized ads and target a specific public by selecting the appropriate characteristics in terms of demographics, interests, behavior, and relationships. This is shown in Figure 8.19. Advertisements are displayed according to a bidding system, where the most eye-catching spots of a page are the most expensive ones. When a user opens his or her Facebook page, a virtual auction decides which ad will be placed where on the page. Depending on the magnitude and the popularity of (a part of) the chosen audience, Facebook suggests a bidding amount. A safer solution is to fix a maximum bid amount in advance. The higher the amount of the bid, the higher the probability of getting a good ad placement. Notice, however, that the winning bid does not necessarily have to pay the maximum bid amount. Only when many ads are competing do ad prices rise drastically. As such, the price of an ad differs depending on the target user.

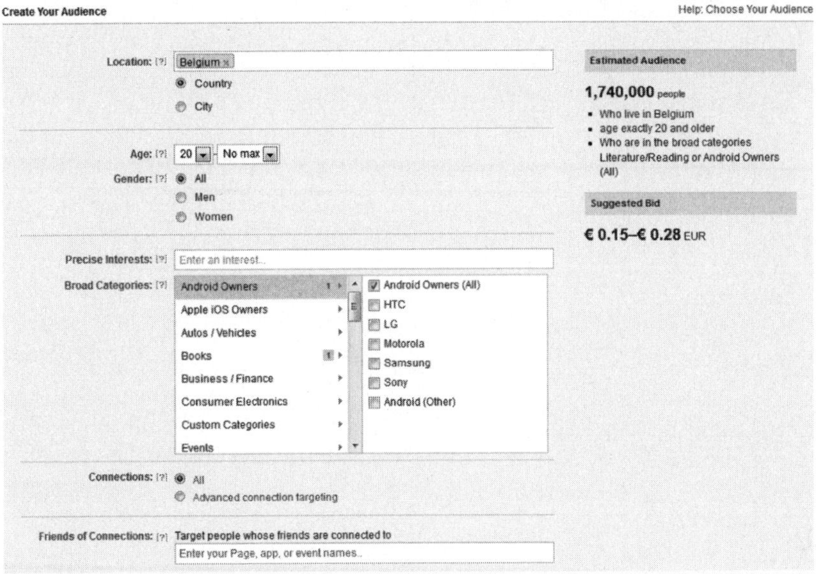

Figure 8.19 Choosing the Audience for Facebook Advertising Campaign

The business-oriented social networking site LinkedIn offers similar services as Facebook. The LinkedIn Campaign Manager[43] allows the marketer to create personalized ads and to select the right customers. Compared to Facebook, LinkedIn Campaign Managers offers services to target individuals based on the characteristics of the companies they are working at and the job function they have (see Figure 8.20). While Facebook Advertising is particularly suitable for Business-to-Consumer (B2C) marketing, LinkedIn Campaign Manager is aimed at advertisements for Business-to-Business (B2B) and Human Resource Management (HRM) purposes.

As most tools are self-explanatory, the reader must be careful when deploying these advertisement tools since they may be so user friendly that the user no longer realizes what he/she is actually doing with them. Make sure that you specify a maximum budget and closely monitor all activities and advertisement costs, definitely at the start of a marketing campaign. A small error can result in a cost of thousands or even millions of dollars in only a few seconds. Good knowledge of all the facilities is essential to pursue a healthy online marketing campaign.

Figure 8.20 LinkedIn Campaign Manager

Sentiment Analysis

Certain social media platforms allow external servers to capture data from a portion of the users. This gateway for external applications is called the API. An API has multiple functions. It offers an embedded interface to other programs. For example, the Twitter API[44] can be used on other sites to identify visitors by their Twitter account. Integrated tweet fields and buttons on web pages allow users to directly post a reaction without leaving the web page. Like buttons are directly connected to your Facebook page through the Facebook API[45] and immediately share the like with all of your friends. However, APIs often permit external servers to connect and mine the publicly available data. Undelimited user-generated content like text, photos, music, videos, and slideshows is not easy to interpret by computer-controlled algorithms.

Sentiment analysis and opinion mining focus on the analysis of text and determining the global sentiment of the text. Before the actual sentiment of a text fragment can be analyzed, text should be

Data Mining and Apps @DataMiningApps 🔒   13 Aug
Data Science rocks!!! Excellent book written by my good friends
Foster Provost and Tom Fawcett!! A must read!

Figure 8.21   Sentiment Analysis for Tweet

preprocessed in terms of tag removal, tokenization, stopword removal, and stemming. Afterward, each word is associated with a sentiment. The dominant polarity of the text defines the final sentiment.

Because text contains many irrelevant words and symbols, unnecessary tags are removed from the text, such as URLs and punctuation marks. Figure 8.21 represents an example of a tweet. The link in the tweet does not contain any useful information, thus it should be removed for sentiment analysis. The tokenization step converts the text into a stream of words. For the tweet shown in Figure 8.21, this will result in:

Data Science / rocks / excellent / book / written / by / my / good / friends / Foster Provost / and / Tom Fawcett / a / must / read

In a next step, stopwords are detected and removed from the sentence. A *stopword* is a word in a sentence that has no informative meaning, like articles, conjunctions, prepositions, and so forth. Using a predefined machine-readable list, stopwords can easily be identified and removed. Although such a stoplist can be constructed manually, words with an IDF (inverse document frequency) value close to zero are automatically added to the list. These IDF values are computed based on the total set of text fragments that should be analyzed. The more a word appears in the total text, the lower its value. This gives:

Data Science / rocks / excellent / book / written / good / friends / Foster Provost / Tom Fawcett / read

Many variants of a word exist. Stemming converts each word back to its stem or root: All conjugations are transformed to the corresponding verb, all nouns are converted to their singular form, and adverbs and adjectives are brought back to their base form. Applied to the previous example, this results in:

Data Science / rock / excellent / book / write / friend / Foster Provost / Tom Fawcett / read

Each word has a positive (+), negative (−) or neutral (o) polarity. Again, algorithms use predefined dictionaries to assign a sentiment to a word. The example contains many positive and neutral words, as shown below:

Data Science / rock / excellent / book / write / friend / Foster Provost / Tom Fawcett / read

    o   +   +   o   o   +   o   o   o

The overall sentiment of the above tweet is thus positive. Although this procedure could easily capture the sentiment of a text fragment, more advanced analysis techniques merge different opinions from multiple users together and are able to summarize global product or service affinity, as well as assign a general feeling toward neutral-polarized words.

Network Analytics

Instead of analyzing user-generated content, network analytics focuses on the relationships between users on social media platforms. Many social media platforms allow the user to identify their acquaintances. Five types of relationships can be distinguished:[46]

1. **Friends.** There is a mutual positive relationship between two users. Both users know each other, and acknowledge the association between them.

2. **Admirers.** A user receives recognition from another user, but the relationship is not reciprocal.

3. **Idols.** A user acknowledges a certain positive connectedness with another user, but the relationship is not reciprocal.

4. **Neutrals.** Two users do not know each other and do not communicate with each other.

5. **Enemies.** There is a negative relationship between two users. Both users know each other, but there is a negative sphere.

Although in most social networking sites only friendship relationships are exploited, Twitter incorporates admirers (followers) and idols (followees) by enabling users to define the people they are interested in. Admirers receive the tweets of their idols. Enemy relationships are not common in social networking sites, except for EnemyGraph.[47] The power of social network sites depends on the true representation of real-world relationships between people. Link prediction is one subdomain of network analytics where one tries to predict which neutral links are actually friendship, admirer, or idol relationships. Tie strength prediction is used to determine the intensity of a relationship between two users.

Homophily, a concept from sociology, states that people tend to connect to other similar people and they are unlikely to connect with dissimilar people. Similarity can be expressed in terms of the same demographics, behavior, interests, brand affinity, and so on. As such, in networks characterized by homophily, people connected to each other are more likely to like the same product or service. Gathering the true friendship, admirer, and idol relationships between people enables marketers to make more informed decisions for customer acquisition and retention. An individual surrounded by many loyal customers has a high probability of being a future customer. Customer acquisition projects should identify those high-potential customers based on the users' neighborhoods and focus their marketing resources on them. This is shown in Figure 8.22(a). However, a customer whose friends have churned to the competition is likely to be a churner as well, and should be offered additional incentives to prevent him or her

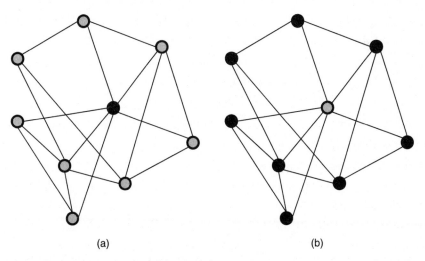

(a) (b)

Figure 8.22 Social Media Analytics for Customer Acquisition (a) and Retention (b). Grey nodes are in favor of a specific brand, black nodes are brand-averse.

from leaving. Similar to customer acquisition, these customers can be detected using relational information available on social media platforms. This is shown in Figure 8.22(b). Influence propagates through the network. The aforementioned analysis techniques focus on the properties of the direct neighborhood (one hop). Although direct associates contain important information, more advanced algorithms focus on influence propagation of the whole network, revealing interesting patterns impossible to detect with the bare eye.

Although social media analytics nowadays is indispensable in companies' market research projects, it is highly advised to verify the regional, national, and international privacy regulations before starting (see privacy section). In the past, some companies did not comply with the prevailing privacy legislation and risked very steep fines.

BUSINESS PROCESS ANALYTICS

In recent years, the concept of business process management (BPM) has been gaining traction in modern companies.[48] Broadly put, the management field aims to provide an encompassing approach in order to align an organization's business processes with the concerns of every involved stakeholder. A business process is then a collection of structured, interrelated activities or tasks that are to be executed to reach a particular goal (produce a product or deliver a service). Involved parties in business processes include, among others, managers ("process owners"), who expect work to be delegated swiftly and in an optimal manner; employees, who desire clear and understandable guidelines and tasks that are in line with their skillset; and clients who, naturally, expect efficiency and quality results from their suppliers. Figure 8.23 gives an example business process model for an insurance claim intake process shown in the business process modeling language (BPMN) standard. Numerous visualization forms exist to design and model business processes, from easy flowchart-like diagrams to complex formal models.

Put this way, BPM is oftentimes described as a "process optimization" methodology and is therefore mentioned together with related quality control terms such as total quality management (TQM), six sigma efforts, or continuous process improvement methodologies.

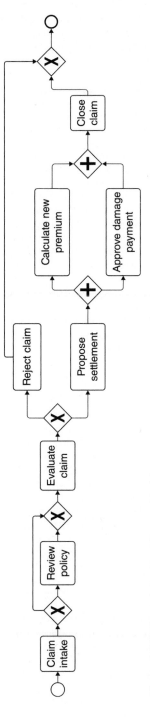

Figure 8.23 Example Business Process Model

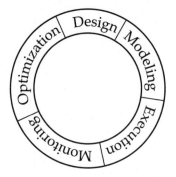

Figure 8.24 Business Process Management Lifecycle

However, this description is somewhat lacking. Indeed, one significant focal point of BPM is the actual improvement and optimization of
processes, but the concept also encompasses best practices toward the
design and modeling of business processes, monitoring (consider for
instance compliance requirements), and gaining insights by unleash-
ing analytical tools on recorded business activities. All these activities
are grouped within the "business process lifecycle," starting with the
design and analysis of a business process (modeling and validation), its
configuration (implementation and testing), its enactment (execution
and monitoring), and finally, the evaluation, which in turn leads again
to the design of new processes (see Figure 8.24).

Process Intelligence

It is mainly in the last part of the BPM life cycle (i.e., evaluation)
where the concepts of process analytics and process intelligence fit in.
Just as with business intelligence (BI) in general, process intelligence
is a very broad term describing a plethora of tools and techniques, and
can include anything that provides information to support decision
making.

As such, just as with traditional ("flat") data-oriented tools, many
vendors and consultants have defined process intelligence to be syn-
onymous with process-aware query and reporting tools, oftentimes
combined with simple visualizations in order to present aggregated
overviews of a business's actions. In many cases, a particular system

will present itself as being a helpful tool toward process monitoring and improvement by providing KPI dashboards and scorecards, thus presenting a "health report" for a particular business process. Many process-aware information support systems also provide online analytical processing (OLAP) tools to view multidimensional data from different angles and to drill down into detailed information. Another term that has become commonplace in a process intelligence context is *business activity monitoring* (BAM), which refers to real-time monitoring of business processes and immediate reaction if a process displays a particular pattern. *Corporate performance management* (CPM) is another popular term for measuring the performance of a process or the organization as a whole.

Although all the tools previously described, together with all the three-letter acronym jargon, are a fine way to measure and query many aspects of a business's activities, most tools unfortunately suffer from the problem that they are unable to provide real insights or uncover meaningful, newly emerging patterns. Just as for non-process-related data sets (although reporting, querying, aggregating and drilling, and inspecting dashboard indicators are perfectly reasonable for operational day-to-day management), these tools all have little to do with real process analytics. The main issues lies in the fact that such tools inherently assume that users and analysts already know what to look for. That is, writing queries to derive indicators assumes that one already knows the indicators of interest. As such, patterns that can only be detected by applying real analytical approaches remain hidden. Moreover, whenever a report or indicator does signal a problem, users often face the issue of then having to go on a scavenger hunt in order to pinpoint the real root cause behind the problem, working all the way down starting from a high-level aggregation toward the source data. Figure 8.25 provides an example of a process intelligence dashboard.

Clearly, a strong need is emerging to go further than straightforward reporting in today's business processes and to start a thorough analysis directly from the avalanche of data that is being logged, recorded, and stored and is readily available in modern information support systems, leading us to the areas of process mining and analytics.

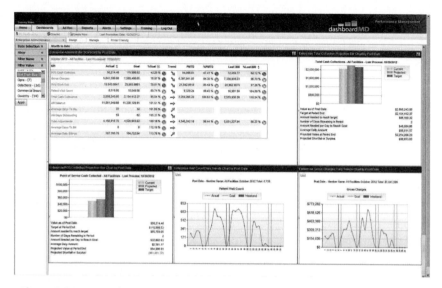

Figure 8.25 Example Process Intelligence Dashboard
Source: http://dashboardmd.net.

Process Mining and Analytics

In the past decade, a new research field has emerged, denoted as "process mining," which positions itself between BPM and traditional data mining. The discipline aims to provide a comprehensive set of tools to provide process-centered insights and to drive process improvement efforts. Contrary to business intelligence approaches, the field emphasizes a bottom-up approach, starting from real-life data to drive analytical tasks.

As previously stated, process mining builds on existing approaches, such as data mining and model-driven approaches, but is more than just the sum of these components. For example, as seen previously, traditional existing data mining techniques are too data-centric to provide a solid understanding of the end-to-end processes in an organization, whereas business intelligence tools focus on simple dashboards and reporting. It is exactly this gap that is narrowed by process mining tools, thus enabling true business process analytics.

The most common task in the area of process mining is called *process discovery*, in which analysts aim to derive an as-is process model starting from the data as it is recorded in process-aware information support systems instead of starting from a to-be descriptive model, and trying to align the actual data to this model. A significant advantage of process discovery is the fact that only a limited amount of initial data is required to perform a first exploratory analysis.

Consider, for example, the insurance claim handling process as it was previously depicted. To perform a process discovery task, we start our analysis from a so-called "event log": a data table listing the activities that have been executed during a certain time period, together with the case (the process instance) to which they belong. A simple event fragment log for the insurance claim handling process might look as depicted in Table 8.4. Activities are sorted based on the starting time. Note that multiple process instances can be active at the same moment in time. Note also that the execution of some activities can overlap.

Based on real-life data as it was stored in log repositories, it is possible to derive an as-is process model that provides an overview of how the process was actually executed. To do this, activities are sorted based on their starting time. Next, an algorithm iterates over all process cases and creates "flows of work" between the activities. Activities that follow each other distinctly (no overlapping start and end times)

Table 8.4 Example Insurance Claim Handling Event Log

Case Identifier	Start Time	Completion Time	Activity
Z1001	8-13-2013 09:43:33	8-13-2013 10:11:21	Claim intake
Z1004	8-13-2013 11:55:12	8-13-2013 15:43:41	Claim intake
Z1001	8-13-2013 14:31:05	8-16-2013 10:55:13	Evaluate claim
Z1004	8-13-2013 16:11:14	8-16-2013 10:51:24	Review policy
Z1001	8-17-2013 11:08:51	8-17-2013 17:11:53	Propose settlement
Z1001	8-18-2013 14:23:31	8-21-2013 09:13:41	Calculate new premium
Z1004	8-19-2013 09:05:01	8-21-2013 14:42:11	Propose settlement
Z1001	8-19-2013 12:13:25	8-22-2013 11:18:26	Approve damage payment
Z1004	8-21-2013 11:15:43	8-25-2013 13:30:08	Approve damage payment
Z1001	8-24-2013 10:06:08	8-24-2013 12:12:18	Close claim
Z1004	8-24-2013 12:15:12	8-25-2013 10:36:42	Calculate new premium
Z1011	8-25-2013 17:12:02	8-26-2013 14:43:32	Claim intake
Z1004	8-28-2013 12:43:41	8-28-2013 13:13:11	Close claim
Z1011	8-26-2013 15:11:05	8-26-2013 15:26:55	Reject claim

will be put in a sequence. When the same activity is followed by different activities over various process instances, a split is created. When two or more activities' executions overlap in time, they are executed in parallel and are thus both flowing from a common predecessor.

After executing the process discovery algorithm, a process map such as the one depicted in Figure 8.26 can be obtained (using the

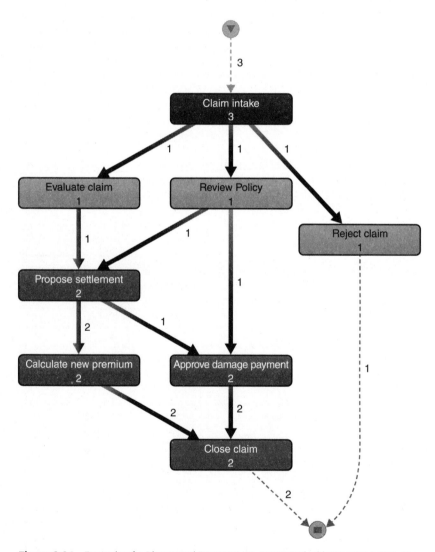

Figure 8.26   Example of a Discovered Process Map Annotated with Frequency Counts

Disco software package). The process map can be annotated with various information, such as frequency counts of an activity's execution. Figure 8.27 shows the same process map now annotated with performance-based information (mean execution time). Note that, together with solid filtering capabilities, visualizations such as these provide an excellent means to perform an exploratory analytics task to determine

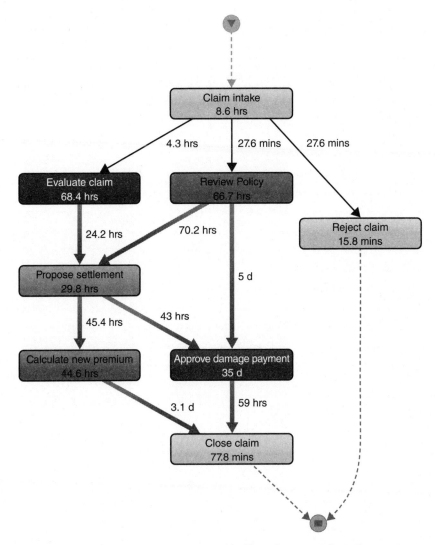

Figure 8.27 Example Process Map Annotated with Performance Information

bottlenecks and process deviations, compared to having to work with flat data–based tools (e.g., analyzing the original event log table using spreadsheet software).

As can be seen from the figures, process discovery provides an excellent means to perform an initial exploratory analysis of the data at hand, showing actual and true information. This allows practitioners to quickly determine bottlenecks, deviations, and exceptions in the day-to-day workflows.

Other, more advanced process discovery tools exist to extract other forms of process models. We discuss here the so-called Alpha algorithm, which was put forward by Wil van der Aalst as one of the first formal methods to extract process models containing split/join semantics, meaning that this discovery algorithm aims to discover explicitly which tasks occur in parallel; in the process maps shown in Figures 8.26 and 8.27, only high level "flows" between activities are depicted, which provides a solid, high-level overview of the process but can be made more specific.[49]

The Alpha algorithm assumes three sets of activities: T_w is the set containing all activities, T_i is the set containing all activities that occur as a starting activity in a process instance (e.g., "claim intake"), and T_o is the set of all activities that occur as an ending activity in a process instance (e.g., "reject claim" and "close claim"). Next, basic ordering relations are determined, starting with $\succ$. It is said that $a \succ b$ holds when activity a directly precedes b in some process instance. Based on this set of orderings, it is said that $a \to b$ (sequence) holds if and only if $a \succ b \land b \nsucc a$. Also, $a \# b$ (exclusion) if and only if $a \nsucc b \land b \nsucc a$ and $a \parallel b$ (inclusion) if and only if $a \succ b \land b \succ a$. Based on this set of relations, a "footprint" of the log can be constructed, denoting the relation between each pair of activities, as depicted in Figure 8.28.

	a	b	c
a	#	→	→
b	←	#	‖
c	←	‖	#

Figure 8.28 Footprint Construction in the Alpha Algorithm

Based on this footprint, it is possible to derive semantic relations between activities:

- $a \rightarrow b$: a and b follow in sequence
- $a \rightarrow b \wedge a \rightarrow c \wedge b \# c$: choice between b or c after a
- $a \rightarrow c \wedge b \rightarrow c \wedge a \# b$: c can follow both after a or b
- $a \rightarrow b \wedge a \rightarrow c \wedge b \parallel c$: b and c are executed both in parallel after a
- $a \rightarrow c \wedge b \rightarrow c \wedge a \parallel b$: c follows after both a and b are executed in parallel

The resulting process model is then shown as a "workflow net," a specific class of Petri nets (see Figure 8.29). Note that the parallelism between "calculate new premium" and "approve damage payment" and the choice between "review policy" and "evaluate claim" are now depicted in an explicit manner.

Process discovery is not the only task that is encompassed by process mining. One other particular analytical task is denoted as *conformance checking*, and this aims to compare an event log as it was executed in real life with a given process model (which could be either discovered or given). This then allows one to quickly pinpoint deviations and compliance problems.

Consider once more our example event log. When "replaying" this event log on the original BPMN model, we immediately see some deviations occurring. Figure 8.30 depicts the result after replaying process instance Z1004. As can be seen, the required activity "evaluate claim" was not executed in this trace, causing a compliance problem for the execution of "propose settlement." Conformance checking thus provides a powerful means to immediately uncover root causes behind deviations and compliance violations in business processes.

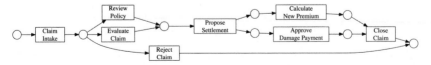

Figure 8.29 Workflow Net for the Insurance Case

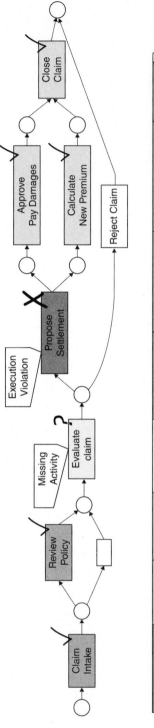

Figure 8.30 Conformance Checking

This concludes our overview of process mining and its common analytics tasks. Note that there exist various other process analytics tasks as well. The following list enumerates a few examples:

- Rule-based property verification of compliance checking (e.g., in an audit context: verifying whether the four-eyes principle was applied when needed)
- Taking into account additional data, other than case identifiers, activity names, and times; for instance, by also incorporating information about the workers having executed the tasks
- Combining process mining with social analytics; for instance, to derive social networks explaining how people work together
- Combining process discovery with simulation techniques to rapidly iterate on what-if experiments and to predict the impact of applying a change in the process

Although Process Mining mainly entails descriptive tasks, such as exploring and extracting patterns, techniques also exist to support decision makers in predictive analytics. One particular area of interest has been the prediction of remaining process instance durations by learning patterns from historical data. Other approaches combine process mining with more traditional data mining techniques, which will be described further in the next section.

Coming Full Circle: Integrating with Data Analytics

The main difference between process analytics (process mining) and data analytics lies in the notion that process mining works on two levels of aggregation. At the bottom level, we find the various events relating to certain activities and other additional attributes. By sorting these events and grouping them based on a case identifier, as done by process discovery, it becomes possible to take a process-centric view on the data set at hand. Therefore, many process mining techniques have been mainly focusing on this process-centric view, while spending less time and effort to aim to produce event-granular information.

Because of this aspect, it is strongly advisable for practitioners to adopt an integrated approach by combining process-centric techniques with other data analytics, as was discussed throughout this book. We

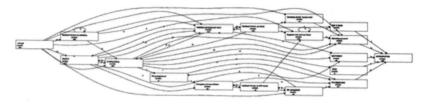

Figure 8.31 Example Spaghetti Model

provide a practical example describing how to do so by integrating process mining and analytics with clustering and predictive decision trees.

To sketch out the problem context, consider a process manager trying to apply process discovery to explore a very complex and flexible business process. Workers are given many degrees of freedom to execute particular tasks, with very few imposed rules on how activities should be ordered. Such processes contain a high amount of variability, which leads process discovery techniques to extract so-called spaghetti models (see Figure 8.31).

Clearly, this is an undesirable scenario. Although it is possible to filter out infrequent paths or activities, one might nevertheless prefer to get a good overview on how people execute their assigned work without hiding low-frequency behavior that may signify both problematic, rare cases and also possible strategies to optimize the handling of certain tasks that have not become commonplace yet. This is an important note to keep in mind for any analytics task: Extracting high-frequency patterns is crucial to get a good overview and derive main findings, but even more important is to analyze data sets based on the impact of patterns—meaning the low frequent patterns can nevertheless uncover crucial knowledge.

Clustering techniques exist to untangle spaghetti models, such as the process model shown, into multiple smaller models, which all capture a set of behavior and are more understandable. One such technique, named ActiTraC, incorporates an active learning technique to perform the clustering, meaning that clusters are created by iteratively applying a process discovery algorithm on a growing number of process instances until it is determined that the derived process model becomes too complex and a new cluster is instantiated.[50] Figure 8.32 shows how the event log previously shown can be decomposed into the following sublogs with associated discovered process models. The

A spaghetti model is obtained after applying process discovery on a flexible, unstructured process:

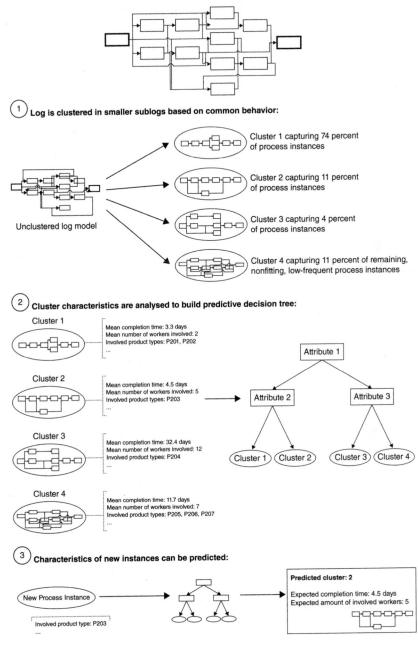

(1) **Log is clustered in smaller sublogs based on common behavior:**

Unclustered log model

Cluster 1 capturing 74 percent of process instances

Cluster 2 capturing 11 percent of process instances

Cluster 3 capturing 4 percent of process instances

Cluster 4 capturing 11 percent of remaining, nonfitting, low-frequent process instances

(2) **Cluster characteristics are analysed to build predictive decision tree:**

Cluster 1
Mean completion time: 3.3 days
Mean number of workers involved: 2
Involved product types: P201, P202
...

Cluster 2
Mean completion time: 4.5 days
Mean number of workers involved: 5
Involved product types: P203
...

Cluster 3
Mean completion time: 32.4 days
Mean number of workers involved: 12
Involved product types: P204
...

Cluster 4
Mean completion time: 11.7 days
Mean number of workers involved: 7
Involved product types: P205, P206, P207
...

Attribute 1

Attribute 2   Attribute 3

Cluster 1   Cluster 2   Cluster 3   Cluster 4

(3) **Characteristics of new instances can be predicted:**

New Process Instance

Involved product type: P203
...

Predicted cluster: 2

Expected completion time: 4.5 days
Expected amount of involved workers: 5

Figure 8.32   Clustering of Process Instances

discovered process models show an easier-to-understand view on the different types of behavior contained in the data. The last cluster shown here contains all process instances that could not be captured in one of the simpler clusters and can thus be considered a "rest" category containing all low-frequency, rare process variants (extracted with ActiTraC plugin in ProM software package).

After creating a set of clusters, it is possible to analyze these further and to derive correlations between the cluster in which an instance was placed and its characteristics. For example, it is worthwhile to examine the process instances contained in the final "rest" cluster to see whether these instances exhibit significantly different run times (either longer or shorter) than the frequent instances.

Since it is now possible to label each process instance based on the clustering, we can also apply predictive analytics in order to construct a predictive classification model for new, future process instances, based on the attributes of the process when it is created. Figure 8.33 shows how a decision tree can be extracted for an IT incident handling process. Depending on the incident type, involved product, and involved department, it is possible to predict the cluster with which a particular instance will match most closely and, as such, derive expected running time, activity path followed, and other predictive information.

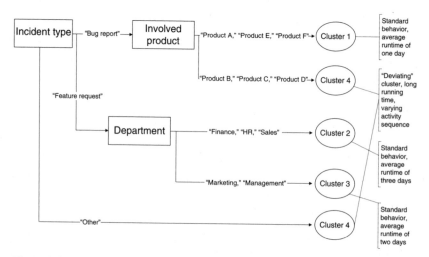

Figure 8.33 Example Decision Tree for Describing Clusters

Decision makers can then apply this information to organize an efficient division of workload.

By combining predictive analytics with process analytics, it is now possible to come full circle when performing analytical tasks in a business process context. Note that the scope of applications is not limited to the example previously described. Similar techniques have also been applied, for example, to:

- Extract the criteria that determine how a process model will branch in a choice point
- Combine process instance clustering with text mining
- Suggest the optimal route for a process to follow during its execution
- Recommend optimal workers to execute a certain task[51] (see Figure 8.34)

As a closing note, we draw attention to the fact that this integrated approach does not only allow practitioners and analysts to "close the

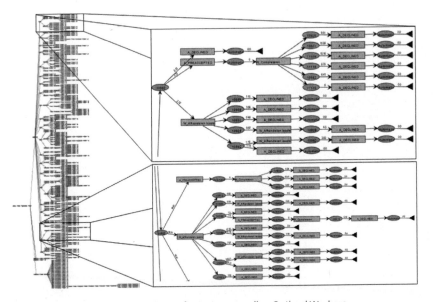

Figure 8.34 Example Decision Tree for Recommending Optimal Workers
Source: A. Kim, J. Obregon, and J. Y. Jung, "Constructing Decision Trees from Process Logs for Performer Recommendation," First International Workshop on Decision Mining & Modeling for Business Processes (DeMiMoP'13), Beijing, China, August 26–30, 2013.

loop" regarding the set of techniques being applied (business analytics, process mining, and predictive analytics), but also enables them to actively integrate continuous analytics within the actual process execution. This is contrary to being limited to a post-hoc exploratory investigation based on historical, logged data. As such, process improvement truly becomes an ongoing effort, allowing process owners to implement improvements in a rapid and timely fashion, instead of relying on reporting–analysis–redesign cycles.

NOTES

1. T. Van Gestel and B. Baesens, *Credit Risk Management: Basic Concepts: Financial Risk Components, Rating Analysis, Models, Economic and Regulatory Capital* (Oxford University Press, 2009); L. C. Thomas, D. Edelman, and J. N. Crook, *Credit Scoring and Its Applications* (Society for Industrial and Applied Mathematics, 2002).

2. B. Baesens et al., "Benchmarking State of the Art Classification Algorithms for Credit Scoring," *Journal of the Operational Research Society* 54, no. 6 (2003): 627–635.

3. T. Van Gestel and B. Baesens, *Credit Risk Management: Basic Concepts: Financial Risk Components, Rating Analysis, Models, Economic and Regulatory Capital* (Oxford University Press, 2009).

4. M. Saerens, P. Latinne, and C. Decaestecker, "Adjusting the Outputs of a Classifier to New a Priori Probabilities: A Simple Procedure," *Neural Computation* 14, no. 1 (2002): 21–41.

5. V. Van Vlasselaer et al., "Using Social Network Knowledge for Detecting Spider Constructions in Social Security Fraud," in *Proceedings of the 2013 IEEE/ACM International Conference on Advances in Social Network Analysis and Mining* (Niagara Falls, 2013). IEEE Computer Society.

6. G. J. Cullinan, "Picking Them by Their Batting Averages' Recency—Frequency—Monetary Method of Controlling Circulation," Manual Release 2103 (New York: Direct Mail/Marketing Association, 1977).

7. V. S. Y. Lo, "The True Lift Model—A Novel Data Mining Approach to Response Modeling in Database Marketing," *ACM SIGKDD Explorations Newsletter* 4, no. 2 (2002).

8. W. Verbeke et al., "Building Comprehensible Customer Churn Prediction Models with Advanced Rule Induction Techniques," *Expert Systems with Applications* 38 (2011): 2354–2364.

9. H.-S. Kim and C.-H. Yoon, "Determinants of Subscriber Churn and Customer Loyalty in the Korean Mobile Telephony Market," *Telecommunications Policy* 28 (2004): 751–765.

10. S. Y. Lam et al., "Customer Value, Satisfaction, Loyalty, and Switching Costs: An Illustration from a Business-to-Business Service Context, *Journal of the Academy of Marketing Science* 32, no. 3 (2009): 293–311; B. Huang, M. T. Kechadim, and B. Buckley, "Customer Churn Prediction in Telecommunications," *Expert Systems with Applications* 39 (2012): 1414–1425; A. Aksoy et al., "A Cross-National Investigation of the Satisfaction and Loyalty Linkage for Mobile Telecommunications Services across Eight Countries," *Journal of Interactive Marketing* 27 (2013): 74–82.

11. W. Verbeke et al., "Building Comprehensible Customer Churn Prediction Models with Advanced Rule Induction Techniques," *Expert Systems with Applications* 38 (2011): 2354–2364.

12. Q. Lu and L. Getoor, "Link-Based Classification Using Labeled and Unlabeled Data," in *Proceedings of the ICML Workshop on The Continuum from Labeled to Unlabeled Data* (Washington, DC: ICML, 2003).

13. C. Basu, H. Hirsh, and W. Cohen, "Recommendation as Classification: Using Social and Content-based Information in Recommendation," in *Proceedings of the Fifteenth National/Tenth Conference on Artificial Intelligence/Innovative Applications of Artificial Intelligence, American Association for Artificial Intelligence* (American Association for Artificial Intelligence, Menlo Park, CA, 1998), 714–720; B. N. Miller et al., "Movielens Unplugged: Experiences with an Occasionally Connected Recommender System," in *Proceedings of the 8th International Conference on Intelligent User Interfaces* (New York, 2003), 263–266. ACM New York, NY, USA.

14. D. Jannach, M. Zanker, and M. Fuchs, "Constraint-Based Recommendation in Tourism: A Multi-Perspective Case Study," *Journal of IT & Tourism* 11, no. 2 (2009): 139–155; F. Ricci et al., "ITR: A Case-based Travel Advisory System," in *Proceeding of the 6th European Conference on Case Based Reasoning, ECCBR 2002* (Springer-Verlag London, UK 2002), 613–627.

15. M. J. Pazzani, "A Framework for Collaborative, Content-Based and Demographic Filtering," *Artificial Intelligence Review* 13, no. 5–6 (1999): 393–408.

16. J. Schafer et al., *Collaborative Filtering Recommender Systems, The Adaptive Web* (2007), 291–324. Springer-Verlag Berlin, Heidelberg 2007.

17. Ibid.

18. Ibid.

19. F. Cacheda et al., "Comparison of Collaborative Filtering Algorithms: Limitations of Current Techniques and Proposals for Scalable, High-Performance Recommender System," *ACM Transactions on the Web* 5, no. 1 (2011): 1–33.

20. J. Schafer et al., *Collaborative Filtering Recommender Systems, The Adaptive Web* (2007), 291–324. Springer-Verlag Berlin, Heidelberg 2007.

21. M. Pazzani and D. Billsus, *Content-Based Recommendation Systems, The Adaptive Web* (2007), 325–341. Springer-Verlag Berlin, Heidelberg 2007.

22. Ibid.

23. R. J. Mooney and L. Roy, "Content-Based Book Recommending Using Learning for Text Categorization," in *Proceedings of the Fifth ACM Conference on Digital Libraries* (2000), 195–204; M. De Gemmis et al., "Preference Learning in Recommender Systems," in *Proceedings of Preference Learning (PL-09), ECML/PKDD-09 Workshop* (2009). ACM, New York, NY, USA 2000.

24. M. Pazzani and D. Billsus, *Content-Based Recommendation Systems, The Adaptive Web* (2007), 325–341. Springer-Verlag Berlin, Heidelberg 2007.

25. A. Felfernig and R. Burke, "Constraint-Based Recommender Systems: Technologies and Research Issues," in *Proceedings of the 10th International Conference on Electronic Commerce, ICEC '08* (New York: ACM, 2008), 1–10.

26. R. Burke, "Hybrid Web Recommender Systems" in *The Adaptive Web* (Springer Berlin/Heidelberg, 2007), 377–408. Springer Berlin Heidelberg.

27. P. Melville, R. J. Mooney, and R. Nagarajan, "Content-Boosted Collaborative Filtering for Improved Recommendations," in *Proceedings of the National Conference on Artificial Intelligence* (2002), 187–192. American Association for Artificial Intelligence Menlo Park, CA, USA 2002.

28. M. Pazzani and D. Billsus, *Content-Based Recommendation Systems, The Adaptive Web* (2007), 325–341.

29. R. Burke, "Hybrid Web Recommender Systems" in *The Adaptive Web* (Springer Berlin/Heidelberg, 2007), 377–408. Springer Berlin Heidelberg.

30. E. Vozalis and K. G. Margaritis, "Analysis of Recommender Systems' Algorithms," in *Proceedings of The 6th Hellenic European Conference on Computer Mathematics & Its Applications (HERCMA)* (Athens, Greece, 2003). LEA Publishers Printed in Hellas, 2003.

31. Ibid.

32. Ibid.

33. G. Linden, B. Smith, and J. York, "Amazon.com Recommendations: Item-to-item Collaborative Filtering," *Internet Computing, IEEE* 7, no. 1 (2003): 76–80.

34. R. J. Mooney and L. Roy, "Content-Based Book Recommending Using Learning for Text Categorization," in *Proceedings of the Fifth ACM Conference on Digital Libraries* (2000), 195–204.

35. D. Jannach, M. Zanker, and M. Fuchs, "Constraint-Based Recommendation in Tourism: A Multi-Perspective Case Study," *Journal of IT & Tourism* 11, no. 2 (2009): 139–155.

36. Ricci et al., "ITR: A Case-based Travel Advisory System," in *Proceeding of the 6th European Conference on Case Based Reasoning, ECCBR 2002* (Springer-Verlag London, UK 2002), 613–627.

37. www.digitalanalyticsassociation.org

38. A. Kaushik, *Web Analytics 2.0* (Wiley, 2010).

39. D. Zeng et al., "Social Media Analytics and Intelligence," *Intelligent Systems, IEEE* 25, no. 6 (2010): 13–16.

40. R. Effing, J. Van Hillegersberg, and T. Huibers, *Social Media and Political Participation: Are Facebook, Twitter and YouTube Democratizing Our Political Systems? Electronic Participation* (Springer Berlin Heidelberg, 2011): 25–35.

41. A. Sadilek, H. A. Kautz, and V. Silenzio, "Predicting Disease Transmission from Geo-Tagged Micro-Blog Data," AAAI 2012.

42. www.facebook.com/advertising

43. www.linkedin.com/advertising

44. http://dev.twitter.com

45. http://developers.facebook.com

46. P. Doreian and F. Stokman, eds., *Evolution of Social Networks* (Routledge, 1997).

47. http://enemygraph.com

48. W. M. P. Van Der Aalst, *Process Mining: Discovery, Conformance and Enhancement of Business Processes* (Springer Verlag, 2011).

49. W. M. P. Van Der Aalst, A. J. M. M. Weijters, and L. Maruster, "Workflow Mining: Discovering Process Models from Event Logs," *IEEE Transactions on Knowledge and Data Engineering* 16, no. 9 (2004): 1128–1142; W. M. P. Van Der Aalst, *Process Mining: Discovery, Conformance and Enhancement of Business Processes* (Springer Verlag, 2011).

50. J. De Weerdt et al., "Active Trace Clustering for Improved Process Discovery," *IEEE Transactions on Knowledge and Data Engineering* 25, no. 12 (2013): 2708–2720.

51. A. Kim, J. Obregon, and Y. Jung, "Constructing Decision Trees from Process Logs for Performer Recommendation," in *Proceedings of the DeMiMop'13 Workshop, BPM 2013 Conference* (Bejing, China, 2013). Springer.

About the Author

Bart Baesens is an associate professor at KU Leuven (Belgium) and a lecturer at the University of Southampton (United Kingdom). He has done extensive research on analytics, customer relationship management, web analytics, fraud detection, and credit risk management (see www.dataminingapps.com). His findings have been published in well-known international journals (e.g., *Machine Learning, Management Science, IEEE Transactions on Neural Networks, IEEE Transactions on Knowledge and Data Engineering, IEEE Transactions on Evolutionary Computation,* and *Journal of Machine Learning Research*) and presented at top international conferences. He is also co-author of the book *Credit Risk Management: Basic Concepts* (Oxford University Press, 2008). He regularly tutors, advises, and provides consulting support to international firms with respect to their analytics and credit risk management strategy.

INDEX